WALKING

WITH

Miss Kay

A Believer's Journey to Glorify God

Bill & Kay Christian

GREEN WINE™
FAMILY BOOKS
a division of
GlobalEdAdvance Press

Walking With Miss Kay
A Believer's Journey to Glorify God
Copyright © 2015 by Bill Christian

Library of Congress Control Number: 2015937717
Walking With Miss Kay
ISBN 978-1-935434-68-9
Bill Christian, 1956 -
Subject Codes and Description: 1: REL 012000: Religion: Christian Life - General 2: REL 012070: Religion: Christian Life—Personal Growth; 3: FAM 014000: Family and Relationships: Death, Grief, Bereavement

Cover design by Brian Lane Green

Printed in Australia, Brazil, France, Germany, Italy, Poland, Spain, UK, and USA   Also available on Espresso Book Machine and anywhere good books are sold.

The Press does not have ownership of the contents of a book; this is the author's work and the author owns the copyright. All theory, concepts, constructs, and perspectives are those of the author and not necessarily the Press. They are presented for open and free discussion of the issues involved. All comments and feedback should be directed to the Email: [comments4author@aol.com] and the comments will be forwarded to the author for response.

Order books from www.gea-books.com/bookstore/
or any place good books are sold.

This book is recommended for participants in
Global W.I.N. -- Women's Inter-reliant Network

Published by

GreenWine Family Books ™
a division of GlobalEdAdvance Press
Global Educational Advance, Inc.

This book is dedicated to

My youngest daughter

ADENA

Affectionately known as "Dee"

Her talent and life were lost much too soon;

She will always be remembered.

"I love you never till the end...!" *

MAMA

---

*Editor's Note

"I love you never till the end." This is the good night
expression of Miss Kay as a small child to her parents. How
she came up with this innocent remark and what it means
remains a mystery. Perhaps it was a child repeating a
statement about endless love, but regardless of its creation,
the declaration has stuck as an affectionate expression of
limitless and never-ending love. It appears to be a child-
like expression of forever love and continues to be used by
family and close friends...till the end!

CONTENTS

INTRODUCTION	A LOVE THAT NEVER ENDS	9
FOREWORD		15
CHAPTER 1	BEGINNINGS	17
CHAPTER 2	GLORY BEGUN	21
CHAPTER 3	MY SHADOW	25
CHAPTER 4	BROKEN DREAMS	31
CHAPTER 5	DADDY'S HOME	43
CHAPTER 6	ANGELS UNAWARE	53
CHAPTER 7	SIFTED	61
CHAPTER 8	RETREAT	67
CHAPTER 9	ABIDING	75
CHAPTER 10	VALLEY OF THE SHADOW OF DEATH	89
CHAPTER 11	WHY?	93
CHAPTER 12	GRIEF EXALTED	97
CHAPTER 13	DETOURS	103
CHAPTER 14	THE UNKNOWN	111
CHAPTER 15	HOME	115
CHAPTER 16	RUNNING WITH PATIENCE	119
CHAPTER 17	DEATH CASTS A LONG SHADOW	141
CHAPTER 18	DEALING WITH PERSONAL LOSS	151
EPILOGUE		167
AFTERWORD		173
ABOUT THE AUTHORS		175

WALKING WITH MISS KAY

Introduction

A Love That Never Ends

"I love you never till the end."
—Miss Kay

This book is not solely about the personal struggles of one believer, but the central focus is about the greatness of God in the midst of a life lived. Scripture is clear that the human condition includes *"a few days and full of trouble."* Each individual faces turmoil, hardship and the bitter testing of a personal nature from the pangs of birth to the anguish of death. Added to these physical trials are the struggles of faith. Within the pages of this book, you will find a life that has faced each of these challenges with a simple faith that dared to believe and trust a loving God.

This is not a story with easy outlines for the believer to use to apply to their own challenges. It is a journey of faith, from early childhood health issues, through a lifetime of physical struggles, to the present medical limitations. It is a story that will challenge your spiritual perspectives about how you view personal trials. Within this journey, it is my prayer that those who walk with Miss Kay will be encouraged in their own journey. Not by applying suggestions as to how to face trials, but by witnessing a life that has lived in the depths of hardship only to realize that God is for us and in us doing a work that is truly a Divine masterpiece! Personal hardships and trials are not about how we feel about the struggle; it is about what God is doing within us through each step of the way.

To know Miss Kay, to have witnessed her life is to call into question why such a sweet, kind and gentle person would be called upon to suffer so much. Yet, unmistaken is the great faith that has been refined in the fires of a life lived with an expectation of God doing great and mighty things. Miss Kay and I join Saint Paul in declaring, *For I consider the sufferings we now endure not worthy to be compared with the glory about to be revealed in us.* (Romans 8:18 EDNT)

May you walk with Miss Kay through her journey, and as you do, may you be encouraged to see God in a new and different perspective. He is not only the Savior from past sins, but He is also the ever present Redeemer of our lives. It is our heartfelt desire that you enter into a relationship with Christ Jesus and know that His only thoughts toward you are of peace and those that bring about His expected end. An end that is the completeness of His will and purpose for your life!

Buried deeply in the Book of Jeremiah (29:11), the weeping Prophet, reproduced the impression I have of our loving Heavenly Father when it comes to my wife, Miss Kay: *"For I know the thoughts that I think toward you, saith the Lord, thoughts of peace, and not of evil (calamity), to give you an expected end (a future and a hope)."* To walk with Miss Kay and witness her life is to call into question why such a sweet,

kind and gentle person would be called upon to suffer so
much. Yet, unmistaken is the great faith that has been refined
in the fires of a life lived with an expectation of God doing
great and mighty things.

Witnessing a person that you love and admire suffer is
one of the most difficult things you can ever experience. Kay is
a very special lady and she has a heart unlike any person that
I have ever known. Her personality is one of the most sincere,
honest and unstained by this world I have witnessed. She is
the type of person that just opens her heart up to others no
matter what their standing in society or what their problems
may be. She knows only one kind of approach to people:
love them with everything she has and if she gets hurt in the
process, then so be it!

Miss Kay's spirit is one of perseverance and one that
approaches issues with a sense of grace not often found
in this world. The fires of life have refined her and God's
grace has molded her into the treasured show piece of His
workmanship. I know no other person personally that has so
impacted God's Kingdom more than Kay has on an individual
basis!

Kay's entire life is a ministry, a service to others! As an
example, a few years ago she shared with me a burden about
those who worked in the doctor's offices where she often
had to visit. She shared that so many times she witnessed
one person after another come into the office and were so
negative and always sharing all the hurts and difficulties with
the staff. So, God laid it upon her heart to go into those offices
and minister to the doctor's staff. Her approach was to go into

the office with a smile on her face and only positive remarks to the staff. I cannot begin to describe the many times I watched her go into a doctor's office and reach out to the staff. By the time we would leave, the entire staff had been refreshed! They had experienced God's grace through a child of God that dared to be different. They had just entertained God's representative and His presence had been known! How many believers would ever think of using their sickness as a tool for ministry? I have not experienced anyone else with that kind of insight or commitment to bear the marks of Christ in their life!

I have been blessed to be a spectator and participant in her life! Kay is one of those types of people that instantly have an impact on you at the first meeting. Not loud and boisterous, but humble and gentle. Her soul is soft and peaceful and if you have an intimate relationship with Christ, you will know right away that this lady has walked with Jesus...often!

Being a spectator through all the trials and through all the suffering, I have come to realize so much more about God's grace. I was taught the fundamental lesson that there is a grace for each day and there was no need to worry about tomorrow, because the grace experienced now is for today, and tomorrow God's grace will be there as needed.

Witnessing Kay's growth as a believer has also challenged me to dig deeper to serve and live out my faith. By that I mean that service is the believer's faith in action. Kay's life has not been about herself, it has been about serving others! Many times that service has been carried out through many small, simple ways, but when put together make them profound. This has been a life lived not to glorify self, but to glorify the One she calls Savior. Kay has truly understood the teachings of Christ concerning how the spiritual life should be lived. She has lived her life as a conduit of God's love and grace to others.

I could write a book on the many lessons that I learned at the footstool of my dear Miss Kay. My prayer is that as you read her story that you too will be impacted by this remarkable lady. May you also know the joy of letting go and letting God have complete control of your life. Then and only then will you know what it is to experience Christ and His sufferings! — **Bill Christian**

Most New Testament references in this book are from the EVERGREEN Devotional New Testament (EDNT). Since the NT content means exactly what the first people who heard it understood it to mean, the EDNT is the result of (42) yeas of dedication to the original intent of Greek words. What did the word mean "then" and is best expressed "now" to benefit the devotional understanding of the New Testament. Miss Kay and I were Patrons to assist the publication of the EDNT and recommend it to you. Obtain your copy of the EDNT by ordering it from the online bookstore at www.gea-books.com or anywhere good books are sold. **Ask for the Complete Edition (2015) — ISBN 978-1-9354349-26-9.**

WALKING WITH MISS KAY

FOREWORD

The best and most beautiful things in the world
cannot be seen or even touched -
they must be felt with the heart.
—Helen Keller

We all drove to Nashville the day before Kay and Carol's surgery. Everyone seemed to have peace – the peace that God promises. Everyone was up and ready to go. We had to be at the hospital early. When we arrived at the hospital, Hannah and I sat in the waiting room. Even though my heart was at peace, there was a dread that I could not explain, but I knew I had to be strong, because God's Word tells us in Joshua 1:9, "Be strong and of a good courage." I had to refuse to be weak. I had to trust and obey no matter what and I knew God was in control and He was going to take care of everything.

There was a TV monitor in the waiting area that kept you updated on everyone in surgery. They were starting with Kay first to be sure they could do the transplant. We were sitting anxiously waiting. Everyone seemed to have God's sweet grace upon them, and I am sure each one of us had a prayer in our hearts. I looked at the monitor and the update was "Carol Pickle in surgery." Then ... "Surgery going well." If

Carol was in surgery, we knew Kay was getting a kidney and we all got excited. I had to give thanks to God.

We got the news that surgery was over for Carol and she was doing fine. Soon after that, surgery was over for Kay and everything was going well. We were able to go see Kay in the recovery room and tell her the good news – she had a new kidney and everything was looking good. That was the most wonderful words a mother could say to a daughter who had suffered so much for so long.

Telling Kay she had a new kidney was similar to when Christ went to the Cross and died for us and He said, "**It is finished**." I praise God for His finished work and His glory and I can never thank Him enough for what He has done for my daughter, Kay. I especially thank Him for sending Don, Carol & family into our lives because I truly believe they were God sent.   God tells us in His Word, to "be still and know that I am God", and it just amazes me how God was looking out for us when we did not even realize it. God's sweet grace was upon us all. **— Georgia, Miss Kay's Mother**

1

BEGINNINGS

*It's wonderful to climb the liquid mountains of the sky.
Behind me and before me is God,
and I have no fears.*

—Helen Keller

*18. For I consider the sufferings we now endure
not worthy to be compared with the glory about
to be revealed in us. 19. All creation is yearning
expecting to see the appearance of the children
of God. 20. For all creation was made subject to
putrefaction, not willingly, but by reason of hope
that it would be redeemed, 21. because creation
itself will be delivered from the bondage of
corruption into the glorious freedom that belongs
to the children of God. 22. Creation and human
beings suffer together until the present. 23. And
not only them, but also the believers of today,
who are the first harvest of the Spirit, even we
ourselves whimper waiting the full adoption, the
redemption of the body. 24. For in hope were we
saved: but hope is waiting for something we do
not yet possess, so if a man possess hope why
does he yet hope? 25. But if we hope for that we
see not, then do we with enduring patience wait
for it. 26. In the same manner the Spirit supports
our weaknesses: for we know not what we should*

pray for as we ought: but the Spirit Himself makes
intercession for us with groans too deep for words.
27. And God who searches all hearts knows
the mind-set of the Spirit, because He makes
intercession for the saints according to the will of
God. 28. We know for those loving God that He
continually works all things together for good, to
those who are the called ones according to His
purpose. (Romans 8:18-28 EDNT)

Ever wonder why you go through the trials of life? Ever see others suffering, knowing the greatness of their faith, and yet wonder why would God allow such a strong believer to suffer as they do? The passage above sheds light on why God allows believers to suffer. It is one of the most straight forward passages in the New Testament that addresses these and other issues which humans face concerning sufferings. Yet it is one of the most undervalued and misinterpreted passages that addresses this vast area of a believer's life.

Let's take a moment to understand and better explain this passage. Paul states that all of creation is crying out in its sufferings. We groan under the tremendous pressure of this thing called life. We have known firsthand the power of His redemption! We have come to know that life is one of hope; hope of future eternity with God in the place which He Himself has prepared for us! But this passage also deals with the limitations of those who have been redeemed. Those limitations are found in verse 26 and they are known as "infirmities."

But what are these infirmities? Translated, they refer to weaknesses, an inability to produce a desired result, a defect or flaw within our own bodies and personalities. What is it that brings so much suffering into our lives? Is it just the physical suffering of life or is it the spiritual warfare that every believer must wage? The true sufferings of this life are defined within this text.......weaknesses within us. Weaknesses that limit our understanding of God, limit our own understanding and of others around us. Weaknesses that crowd out understanding and blur the vision of what God is doing in our lives at each moment.

How do weaknesses limit us? Put this into the context of Paul's writing. He speaks of believers and the struggles they go through. Our spiritual lives were built upon the hope that is found in Christ, but the problem is that the present has difficulties and trials that our future cannot defeat. We look through the course of time, holding onto that grand, glorious future that God has for us, but the problems and sufferings still have to be confronted. We groan within ourselves; calling out to God in prayer and, probably praying that God will remove the hardships so that we can only experience His blessings. And as we do, we are missing the point of vs. 26. God has given to every believer the Holy Spirit as a personal guide to comfort and teach us the purpose that God has for us.

This verse teaches us that when we do not know what to pray for ourselves or our circumstance, then the Holy Spirit intercedes for us in lifting up prayers on our behalf, according to God's plan and purpose. This intercession is God intervening in our lives, helping us to understand His will and to embrace all that is going on within our lives to get the full message of His grace!

Living is not about getting out of suffering; it is about trusting God through the suffering and knowing that He is with us through every turn in the journey. God is not just a God of the blessed times, but He is a God who is with us at all times......even those times of great suffering and conflict.

It is in this course of the journey that we pick up Miss Kay's life. In order to truly understand her journey with God, you must first understand the costs of that journey. Without knowing some of the issues that she has faced, it is hard to understand the lessons of grace that she has been blessed to learn and share with others. So we enter into her present life and discover a middle aged daughter, sister, wife, mother, grandmother, educator, Sunday school teacher, deaf interpreter and speaker on women's issues. We find Miss Kay walking with God each day enjoying His presence and learning fresh lessons of grace.

The following chapters will address this wonderful lady's life and journey with God. Much of this story will be in her words; other parts will be in the words of those who have been blessed to interact with her. God has a purpose for you in reading this story and in sharing with you the great and mighty things He has done through this child of His. Come take a walk with Miss Kay!

2

GLORY BEGUN

Grace is but glory begun,
and glory is but grace perfected.
—Jonathan Edwards

Being a mother and grandmother, I look back over my life with a great deal of wonder! I am amazed at how my Heavenly Father has brought me through so many difficult times to where I am now. His grace is greater than my words to describe His deeds and His mercy is beyond my imagination. The words I share with women's groups is the best way to explain His favor: **God has grace for each day, for every situation encountered in our lives!** That is my God's grace; there every day and at every crossroad of life. Whether the road has been rocky, steep with dangerous cliffs or smooth rolling hills, God's grace has been there to sustain me and guide me, step by step.

My story is not so dissimilar from many of the readers of this book, yet, it is unusual. I am a firm believer that Saint Paul speaks clearly to this issue:

13. No test has come your way but such as is common to man: God is faithful, who will not permit you to be tempted beyond your endurance; but will with each test also show you a way of escape, so that you may be victorious (1 Corinthians 10: 13 EDNT).

      Our troubles and trials are alike in many ways. Yet, certain trials hit us when we least expect them, or when we are at our weakest point. These tests may be similar to trials gone through by others, but when they hit us they seem worse. I suppose each person thinks their cross is the hardest to endure.

      Even though personal trials are similar to those of others, individual suffering has a different purpose with respect to what God is doing in each life. My experiences with illness and disease were used by the Holy Spirit to produce spiritual growth in ways I did not understand at the time. God had a plan for me even though I did not understand it. He had a purpose for each episode of my life and how He wanted to use me. My life was but a canvas and He was the Master Artist that would bring beauty, color, and detail to His creation!

      As God's children, we will not always understand the seasons of trial and suffering that we go through. We attempt to put God in a corner so that we can force Him to divulge His purpose. Yet, our Heavenly Father is not so easily contained, nor is He one that will bend to our will. His purpose may appear to be hidden, or even mysterious. Why does God hide His intention when performing a work in our lives? There are many reasons why God does not reveal His will according to our time table.

      First, in my life, His purpose would be revealed through a timeline of years, not days, weeks or months. His spiritual lessons of patience, perseverance and endurance were teachings that He utilized later in my life. As disease and illness began to take control of my body and dominate my life, these spiritual instructions would be guidance toward His desired destination. As my physical limitations increased, my spirit would know the freedom that had been seasoned with the fires of trial.

Grace is but glory begun, and glory is but grace perfected, as quoted from Jonathan Edwards, describes the seasoning of grace in the believer's life. Grace for every need; grace for each trial. Grace is God's glory being perfected in our lives! **Feeling the pains of sickness or the sorrow of failure is how God utilizes our weakness to mature us in His grace.** In each situation, God creates a catalog of experiences that will benefit us the rest of our lives. These experiences, one connected to another, become the total of individual graces we have been blessed to experience. Each grace is but a piece of God's invested blessing within us! Each grace is one aspect of His character being implanted within our souls to be drawn upon at a later time in order that we might fully know Him and the perfection of His grace!

Richard L. Evans once said, *"Don't let life discourage you; everyone who got where he is had to begin where he was."* I trust you would gain from this chapter exactly what Evans said. Life is filled with discouraging moments, trials, sorrows, tragedies and sufferings; but we must not be discouraged on our journey! We must begin where we are, work with what we have and go with God's plan from that place forward! This does not mean that the load will be lightened, nor does it mean that the burden will be easier; it simply means that we must learn to rely totally on God and the special grace He has designed for us daily in each circumstance.

How is it that believers trust God with their eternal life, but cannot trust Him with their daily lives? Shall those who are the handiwork of the Master take cause with His choice or manner of perfection? Grace is intended for our benefit and God's glory! Can those who are dead to sin, dead indeed unto them-selves, rise from their sick bed to criticize God's way of perfection? In the vastness of God's creation, He selected man to be the trophy of His grace! He chose us to be the bearer of His marks of faith! He has taken His brush, selected the colors that most accent our lives, and chose the portrait that we will become! How can we resist the Hand of God upon canvas of our lives?

3

MY SHADOW

*Trials teach us what we are; they dig up the soil,
and let us see what we are made of.*

—Charles Spurgeon

*9. And God said, my grace is sufficient for you:
for my strength is made perfect in weakness.
Most gladly therefore will I rather boast in my
weaknesses, that the power of Christ may rest
upon me. 10. I take pleasure, therefore, in my
weakness, ill-treatment, necessary hardships,
troubles and difficulties, when they are distresses
for Christ's sake: for when I am weak, then am I
strong. (2 Corinthians 12:9-10 EDNT)*

I was diagnosed as a juvenile diabetic at age 10. My
Mother, Georgia, began to notice certain symptoms that led
her to believe that I might be diabetic. Our family doctor
diagnosed diabetes and the shots began! Diabetes affected
me in ways that most people do not realize. Certainly, I had
to change some things: my diet changed, I was now on insulin
every day to remain active and healthy, but those were not the
only changes.

Now I had to check my sugar levels daily and even
weigh the food that I ate. I could no longer just skip a meal, my

food intake was important. One of the issues that presented a problem early on was my sugar dropping, which would lead to me having to take orange juice or something sweet to get my sugar back to normal. This really impacted the way I lived and how I went about my daily life. Diabetes made it difficult to have a normal adolescent life. Birthday parties, where I would normally be able to eat cake and ice cream were now off limits. Diabetes had begun a life time assault on my body and general health.

When I was in the seventh grade, I experienced my first diabetic coma. As a teenager, my illness was getting out of control. My doctor worked all night trying to bring me through this life-threatening episode. This would be the beginning of the harsh stage of my journey and my battle with diabetes.

Few people actually understand the tremendous stress diabetes puts on the body. The disease attacks small blood vessels throughout the body. The first organ that receives major damage is the pancreas, then the disease moves on to the kidneys, eyes, lower limbs, nerve endings, heart, brain, etc. It has been estimated that the greatest amount of damage from diabetes is done within the first 11 years of the disease. For most people, that damage is done before they even know they have the disease! When I started my battle with diabetes there were no blood monitors to check blood levels at home. We just did not have all the options to control diabetes that exist today. Diabetic troubles for me in those days were non-stop and unrelenting!

Diabetes would be my shadow throughout my teen and early adult years. Each passing year brought more hospital visits, more extensive treatments, more tests, more damage to my body, and more general health problems. The assault was one that my body would resist for the first 15 years with great resolve. My body's strength was tested over and over, but with each set back, my body would bounce back and again regain its strength and move on toward healing. What was unknown to all of us was what was going on inside my body. Each organ, each group of small blood vessels would be damaged more and more with each passing set back.

Disease and suffering that comes with diabetes are a part of many lives either directly or indirectly. Some are directly impacted by the disease and others have a loved one with a developing disease. We have all felt the results of disease and suffering. One of the hardest questions for believers is to ask: what good comes out of such suffering? Does God have a reason for each episode or stage of a disease?

Paul, in his second letter to the Corinthian believers dealt with this issue. Paul wrote:

> 3. Praise God, even the Father of our Lord Jesus Christ, the Father of compassion, and the God who stands beside you to encourage; 4. Who stands beside us to encourage during any kind of affliction that we in turn may be able to encourage others every time afflictions arise, by the consolation we received of God. 5. As the sufferings of Christ overflows to us, our consolation and encouragement flows from Christ. 6. And if we have miserable problems, it is for your reassurance and deliverance, that if you suffer the same difficulties you can be encouraged that we

were made free from worry to the effect that you can be delivered. 7. Our hope is firmly grounded in you, knowing, that as you share in our sufferings you will also share in our encouragement (2 Corinthians 1:3-7 EDNT).

Paul is teaching in this passage that tribulations are meant to make us usable for the Kingdom. God comforts us when we enter into tribulations (times of being pressured, or distressed), but He does not comfort us just so that we will feel better or just go on with living our lives. God comforts us in order that we might be able to comfort someone else when they enter into a time of testing. Notice he states in vs. 4. *Who stands beside us to encourage during any kind of affliction that we in turn may be able to encourage others every time afflictions arise, by the consolation we received of God.* This links believers directly to God's intentions in comforting us. He does not comfort us so that we will lay that experience aside, but so that we can draw upon that experience when we witness another believer going through the same type of suffering.

I am certain God did not bring this disease upon me, but He did allow it to come my way because He had another objective in mind. That objective was experience as explained by Paul in (Romans 5):

1. Since we stand declared righteous by faith, let us enjoy the possession of peace with God through our Lord Jesus Christ: 2. by whom we have access by faith into the grace wherein we stand, and we rejoice in the hope of God's glory. 3. And not only, but we also glory in hardships and sufferings: because we know that troubles produce patient

endurance; 4. and patient endurance approves
character; and character brings hope: 5. and a
faithful trust in God's promises will never put us to
shame; because the love which God has for us is
poured out in abundance in our hearts by the Holy
Spirit which is God's gift (Romans 5:1-5 EDNT).

In the midst of tribulations, the believer can give glory to our Heavenly Father......why? Because He is working suffering and trials into His plan for our lives! Those trials produce an attitude of perseverance and stubborn persistence that builds character within us. This is Christ-like character, not worldly character. This type of character is one that is submissive and humble in its approach to God. Character produces hope or faith, and this faith is not ashamed to be identified with the risen Christ! This type of faith does not disappoint the grace of God but bends itself toward God's grace in order for His purpose to be utilized in the believer's life!

As believers, when we go through sufferings, even though the tribulation was not sent by God, He interacts with the tribulation to produce a divine work! One area of victory is when we come to realize that God's purpose is interwoven in every aspect of our lives! Think about how your perspective of difficulties will change with this understanding.

In the midst of each personal trial, God is working through His Holy Spirit to mature us, to grow us, to take us through this process that Paul spoke of in Romans 5. This process is one that must be accomplished if we are to move toward God and His purpose for us. This process is normally painful. There are times when certain stages of the process will be repeated either because we have not learned the life-lesson or because God has more refining to do so that we might become a useful vessel of honor!

Each of us has our shadows that go where we go; however, as we enter into the process of perseverance, character, and hope, may we learn well the life-lessons of our time aided by the Holy Spirit. These lessons are designed by God to shape and mold us into the image of His Son! As Warren Wiersbe said, *We must never think that patience is complacency. Patience is endurance in action.*

After high school, God would lead me into marriage and motherhood. There again, my shadow would rise up to assault me and ravage my body in a new and heart-wrenching way. Entering into my first pregnancy everything seemed to be going so well. Until one Sunday evening, my seventh month of pregnancy, a simple virus would send me into labor.

4

Broken Dreams

*If you begin to live life
looking for the God that is all around you,
every moment becomes a prayer.*
—Frank Bianco

*6. Herein you are triumphant, even if it is
presently necessary to be saddened by trials of
many sorts, 7. this must be so you can give proof
of your faith, a more precious thing than gold
tested by fire, this proof will bring you praise, and
glory, and honor when Jesus Christ is revealed. 8.
You never saw Him, but you learned to love Him,
although you do not see Him, you believed in
Him. And rejoice with triumphant joy. 9. You are
receiving that which faith ultimately brings, the
salvation of the soul (1 Peter 1:7-9 EDNT)*

We entered the hospital not really knowing what was
happening. The nurses thought it was just false labor. They
assured us that there was no need to worry. The baby seemed
fine and I seemed to be responding to treatment. Then, my
water broke and it would set in motion a series of events that
would forever change our lives!

Our first baby was born at 7:00 AM, on March 7, 1977! Weighing only 4 pounds and 15 ounces, she was so tiny and in such deep trouble! The doctors informed us that she actually weighed only about 1.5 to 2 pounds, and that the rest of her weight was fluid from my diabetes. She was instantly put into the critical care unit for newborns. Her outcome looked bleak. The doctors wanted to run a spinal tap that would help determine if there was any damage to her brain function. The first test drew blood, which meant she was hemorrhaging in her brain. The next day, another spinal tap was run; this test did not show any signs of hemorrhaging. We were thankful.

Emotions at first were so mixed. Was our baby daughter OK or was the second test misleading? The doctors could give us no firm conclusions, so we were told to wait and see! Waiting is not one of the most popular traits of most human beings. We were living in the "micro-wave" age and we wanted to know "now" and the sooner the better! Mothers are not patient when it comes to their children. The maternal nature of caregivers is programmed with the desire that children be healthy and whole. However, the journey as parents is not without surprises, nor is it without curves, bumps and even pot-holes in the road. Around each turn parents face a newness that will impact their lives in many ways. Spiritually, the real question is not how bad is the situation, but how will I respond to this incident.

At feeding time, they would bring the babies out briefly for the new mothers to feed them. I remember Amber having all these IV's hooked up to her; she was jaundiced and was under warming lights. She was very sick and could not eat; it seemed that tubes were everywhere. Her little hands looked like bird claws. My grandmother, Lulu, worked in the nursery and was a big help during this time. She helped me to understand everything that was going on with Amber and what the nurses and doctors were doing.

At first, I could only look through the window to see the babies. I remember when they would bring the babies out to the mothers at feeding time, I would walk down to the nursery and look in and just watch my baby girl. After a while, they would let me and Bill start scrubbing up, going in with gloves, gown and a mask to sit by her at the incubator. We were able to open the little port hole window and just touch her little hand. During the time between these short visits with Amber, I would go to the bathroom and just cry, so yearning to hold my baby girl.

When Amber was about a week old, I finally got to hold her! I held her carefully due to the tubes, IV's, and all the monitors attached to determine her vitals. It was such a thrill to hold my daughter for the first time! My grandmother helped put her in my lap, and of course it was scary.

When the hospital discharged me, Amber had to stay. I would go and feed her twice a day on my own, and then when Bill got off from work, we would go together and feed her supper. She had special feeding tubes instead of a bottle because she could not drink even an ounce at that time. We had to help her do that by squeezing the little nipple, because she couldn't suck hard enough to get the milk. As the days and weeks came and went, she began to progress and started to get better.

Things looked good, and they were waiting for her weight to increase, but they would not let her come home until she was at least five pounds. The first thing every morning I would call and ask "What does Amber weigh this morning?" I remember when we started getting close, during that last week, she was 4 pounds, 15 ounces, then she would go down to 4 pounds, 13 ounces. I'd be either excited, or like "Oh, man!" because she would tend to lose a little here and there. Then the day dawned when we finally got to bring her home!

At that time, we were not aware that there had been a stroke or that any birth defects existed. One of the first problems I noticed was that I had a hard time getting diapers on her; I almost had to pry her legs apart. They sent us to an orthopedic doctor who put a big pillow (hip brace) in between her legs; they said her hip joints were dislocated and that the pillow would take care of it. She had to use the brace for the longest time and it was hard to dress her, because of the big pillow! It kept her legs in a wide-open position to put the hip joints back in socket. She wore the brace several months. When we finally got the OK to remove the hip brace, we thought, "Okay, now everything is fine!"

Then I noticed she kept her left hand closed almost all of the time, and her thumb tucked under her fingers. At first the doctor said it was a ligament that needed to be popped, and if it did not release on its own, they would do surgery. I also noticed she could not sit up on her own. Her doctor stated even though she was a year old by now, it was due to her hip being dislocated for so long. It seemed constantly that things just did not seem right. She could not crawl and I just really started getting discouraged with all the issues. Somebody advised us to go to a different doctor, and when we did, he said, "Yes, all of these things are wrong, but it is because she has cerebral palsy!"

As a nineteen-year-old mother, I went to the doctor by myself, which was the normal routine. I was not expecting anything traumatic. Then the doctor asked, "Do you know what cerebral palsy is?" All I could say was, "No, I don't." He explained, "Somewhere along the line of her premature birth, she had some brain damage." Later on we found out that she had a stroke at birth, and that was what caused the brain damage. The doctor continued, "At this point, I can't tell you if your daughter will ever walk, if she'll ever talk, if she'll feed herself.......I just don't know. She may do all those things; she may not be able to do any of those things........it's too early to tell."

I remember leaving the doctor's office completely devastated! I went to where Bill worked and told him everything the doctor had shared with me. We both just sat there in the car crying. He got off work and came home to be with me. That day will forever be ingrained into our hearts! It was a day of shock, sadness, depression, and feelings of great apprehension! Fear of the unknown! What would the future be for our little girl? As young as we both were, how could we ever meet her special needs?

Not long after that, I was at home washing dishes. Looking out the window, I was having a pity party and asked "God, why? I don't understand." I was so young and so scared.

This was the first time I ever questioned God about our baby girl! It seemed God spoke to my heart in such a strong way. "I chose you to take care of her because I knew she needed someone for her special needs. I knew she would need extra help, and I chose you! And now that I have chosen you, I have expectations for you to do what I have called you to do with this needy child." It may sound crazy, but I had a peace about it; not knowing what would happen, I still had a peace about it. This would be the last time I would ever question God about Amber! He had given me such a total peace that I never had another doubt about His intensions and purpose for our daughter. His peace was both sure and it became an anchor to my soul. It held me and comforted me in ways that are hard to explain.

Bill and I have been blessed by Amber's progress! She finally started crawling, but she had her own way of crawling. The fine motor skills in her left hand were extremely poor, so we started taking her to the Palmer Center in Kingsport, which is a center for handicapped children. She went there for physical therapy, and that is where we learned our daily routine of PT! They would teach me the therapy routine and on the days we didn't go to the center, I would do PT at home. I remember getting up, starting Amber's PT by pushing her legs, stretching the leg muscles and working her hand. Every day we went through the routine; praying and believing, "Today's the day she'll take that first step!" The daily PT was on going. It was our special time together and would later help Amber in many ways!

Amber did finally walk, but she walked on her tiptoes and would stand on her tiptoes with her knees together. She couldn't sit normally. She would sit with her knees folded underneath her basically sitting on the calves of her legs. We found out that the cerebral palsy had impacted her hamstrings. They were so tight that she couldn't stretch her legs straight out. When she tried to stand straight up, her hamstrings would keep her calves from flexing, and she could not fully extend her legs or sit normally.

Her doctor told us the only way to help with this problem was to perform surgery. Her first surgery was when she was three-and-a-half years old. The surgery was done on three places on each leg. They operated on the heel, cutting the heel cord in two, stretching it, and then reconnecting it. They operated on the back of her knees, and on her groin area; doing releases to loosen up all those areas. She was put in kind of a half body cast with a bar in-between it.

The surgery was traumatic! We heard her screaming as they were bringing her to her room......with all the pain, she was terrified! She would remain in the body cast for several weeks. Bill and I took care of her the best we could. Lifting her with the body cast on was difficult. After the cast was removed, the doctor explained what was expected of Amber. By this time, Amber was feeding herself and was talking. I remember all these things were such milestones in our life! Later her surgeon would tell me, "I expect Amber to walk, but I expect her to always be on crutches or on a walker, but I do expect her to walk with aid."

Once again, off to therapy we went! Amber sure didn't want to use the tiny walker. As we would work in therapy concerning using the walker, she'd start out with her hands on the walker handles; the next thing I knew, she would drop to her hands and knees and crawl under the bottom bar of the walker! Again, she'd take off crawling in her little way! She just didn't want to use that walker! She seemed to have her own mindset concerning that walker and just refused to learn to walk with it! Little did we know that stubborn spirit was trying to tell us something!

I will never forget her first steps! We were having a fellowship with our youth at church, and of course Amber was with us. Adena, our second child had been born by this time, but she was just a baby. Amber, being 4 years old, was in metal leg braces to aid with her cerebral palsy and, as I looked in Amber's direction, she just began taking steps! My mind was just racing. I'll never forget that day...her first steps! She just started walking; no walker, no crutches, nothing! It seemed like a miracle.

When I took her back to the surgeon, he said "How are we doing?" I said, "Fine." He looked around and said, "Where's her walker?" I said, "She doesn't need it." He looked at me and said, "What?" I shared with him what had happened. I'll never forget the look on his face! He said, "Let's go out in the hall." So we went out in the hall. He stood on one end and we stood at the other end; and Amber walked to him with no aid whatsoever! He truly was amazed! God blessed her so much! She had to have a lot of other surgeries, but she still walks with no aid!

All believers face giants in their lives, the key is how do we respond. We can retreat and run, or we can face the giant. Whether it is a financial giant, a relationship giant or one like our baby girl; we must face the giants in order to gain the victory! Whatever the giant is, God will bless and help if you are willing to trust Him. That trust will lead you to let go and let God! Letting go and letting God is not a simple process, it takes time and is a maturing process. The giants that we face may be uncharacteristic at times. It may be something that we have never encountered before! God uses these giants as opportunities to grow us, to mature us and to teach us life-lessons that we could not learn any other way.

What should be our response when we face one of these spiritual giants? First, retreat is not the answer. Retreat is the response to fear and 2 Timothy 1:7 says, *For God has not given us the spirit of cowardice, but of power and of love and self-control.* This power is overcoming power, and the love is God's love, and the sound mind is a mind that is not controlled by outside sources. God's will is for His children to be controlled by His Spirit, not by forces from the outside.

Those outside sources are the fiery darts (Ephesians 6:16) that Satan always throws our way in order to disable us or to prevent us from fulfilling God's plan for our lives. Those fiery darts are two-fold. First, they are darts, so they have a distinct target. That target is one that Satan knows will inflict great spiritual harm. Second, it's a dart that is set on fire! So it has a distinct target, but it also is on fire, which means it is designed to spread its destruction! Satan's plan of attack is one of direct attack, the dart, and then to spread its damage (the fire) throughout our lives!

2 Corinthians 2:11 *Lest Satan outsmart us: for we know of his schemes.* Satan will always take advantage of our weakness, but when we know of his schemes we can withstand the evil devices. Letting go and letting God is a process that teaches that spiritual responsibility is to release the giant into the hands of God. So, we are not to retreat, but we are to release our burdens, our fears and our inabilities to the Lord so He can defeat our giants. How do we defeat these giants?

- **First, we have to recognize the giants.** We have to face the fact that the giant is too big for us and we cannot defeat Satan alone.

- **Second, we release the weaknesses and inabilities to the Lord in worship.** That release is an act of submission to Christ as the Lord of our lives and allowing Him to be the Lord over the giants. The release, or turning the giants over to the Lord, is releasing our grip on the giant; we're releasing our grip so that the Lord can take over. Kathleen Norris said, "The end of our control......is the beginning of God's reign."

- **Third, we stop trying to rescue our loved one, or the situation.** Whatever the giant is, we have released our grip in order for the Lord to take control. We must stop trying to rescue and enter into God's will.

- **Fourth, we rest in the Lord!** This rest is a spiritual rest, not an earthly rest. It's not about giving up, for letting go and letting God is not giving up. It is trusting God with the precious treasures of our lives and believing Him for the outcome! Our rest is one of trust, not defeat, nor giving up. Letting go and letting God measures our willingness to obey God in the midst of great trials and temptation. The trial could be our situation and the temptation is for us to take control of the giant, to start out on our own agenda. Obedience is God's desire and obedience is the only way to please Him. Dr. Bill Christian: "Letting go and letting God also measures our courage to live where we do not rule." Robert Anthony: "Courage is simply the willingness to be afraid and act anyway."

Spiritual courage is all about living where we do not rule, but Christ does! Letting go is about decisions now, not the end result of tomorrow. Most of us, want everything now. We are impatient by nature and especially when it comes to someone we love, we want the miracle now! But letting go is about living where we do not rule, it is where Christ rules and He rules supreme! That means that we let go of our grip today and put complete trust in the Lord for tomorrow. Again, that's not easy, but it's God's way! God will surprise you when you let go.

WALKING WITH MISS KAY

5

DADDY'S HOME

*In each family, a story is playing itself out,
and each family's story embodies
its hope and its despair.*
—Augustus Napier

As human beings, part of our connectedness has to do
with our links to the past. In most families, there is a strong
sense of family history. Looking back over my childhood, I
realize I am so blessed! My memories of my childhood are
filled with days playing with my friends and my cousins, Mark
and Tony. They lived right next door and we had so many
great times together. My cousin Donna was also a big part
of my childhood. We played Barbie dolls together, rode my
motorcycle (80 cc.....huge) and generally romping through the
neighborhood having a great time. My mom always took me
to church from the time I was an infant. My Dad did not go to
church, but mom was faithful to take me to worship. Growing
up spiritually at Sunnyside Baptist Church has filled my life
with some great memories. My best friend, Sherry Godsey
and I, would often spend the night with each other. We had so
many wonderful hours playing, swinging and just being best
friends. During our teen years, we sang in the youth choir, we

would spend hours together talking about boys and making fun of Bluegrass singing (we sure didn't like Bluegrass).

The youth Pastor, Roger Solomon, was the greatest! He was a converted Jew and it was amazing to hear him play the piano! He and his wife, Patsy, became a powerful influence in my young Christian life! God used them to help mold my life, shape me in ways that today I see as a reflection of the walk they had themselves in the Spirit. They helped guide me through the troublesome teenage years. They were more than just a youth pastor and his wife, they were real friends! They cared about us, they loved us and they were devoted to our spiritual journey! Roger died a few years ago with a heart attack and I can only imagine his entrance into heaven! The joy that I used to witness on his face, the smile that all of "his kids" used to see and the way he could light up a room for Jesus just through his presence! I miss him and one day in the sweetness of my passing, I will see my friend again!

There was also another best friend that truly impacted my childhood days, probably as much as anyone. Her name was Connie Perry and she was my bodyguard in kindergarten! We would go over to her house and she would have parties, sleepovers and we would all just be silly, crazy girls! We used to watch the movie "Your Cheating Heart" about Hank Williams! We'd just cry at the end of it! Those days together were spent being ourselves, enjoying childhood, playing, and of course, picking on boys. We were so mean, but not to each other. This great childhood friendship has followed us all our days. We have always been there for one another in every kind of circumstance, whether good or bad. We have shed a lot of tears together, but we have also enjoyed the gift of laughter. Now we are both mothers and grandmothers, but still best friends.

My mom and dad were such a huge part of my growing up years. My mom and I have always been close and my daddy has always claimed a special place in my heart. Daddy was a big man, standing about 6'4" and weighing about 260 pounds in his prime. He was a contractor running his own crews most of his life. He was just a quiet, giant of a man with a heart as big as he was! He was my protector, provider, my knight and the man who taught me so much about gentleness!

In all my struggles, my dad was always there! He always quietly supported me, caring for me in ways that were special moments between us and always with a hug for his little girl to make everything feel better. Dad was never one to visit me much in the hospital that was not his way. He would always be waiting for me when I came home, usually already having been by the store to buy me some fruit and tomatoes, which was about every weekend in the summer!

Daddy was a man who knew only one way to love, and that was with all his heart! God taught me so much about love through this man. He loved me unconditionally and never made me feel "unimportant." The little things that he did were always wrapped in his love and were meant to make me feel special. My daddy always gave so much of himself to me! He had that gentle spirit, one that was not boastful, just there with its support. That gentle support and big heart helped to carry me through many of the storms that I encountered early in my life.

As I stated before, growing up my mom was the one who always took me to church. My dad was not a Christian when I was growing up and did not accept Christ until a couple of years before he passed away. Like so many people, he had a lot of good qualities, but those special qualities did not mean he was a saint, nor did it mean that he did not need Jesus to get into heaven. And when my dad did accept salvation, what a transformation took place in his life! He truly was a new creation! He was still the same man that I had loved, he still had that kind and gentle spirit, but there was so much more that had been added to his life. Christ coming into his life gave my dad a whole new perspective about life and living. And that salvation would be the strength that would help him to face the biggest challenge of his life ...death!

Dad had been having a small growth in his throat cut out each year for several years. His doctor told him that they wanted to give him radiation treatment after the last surgery so this growth would not come back. However, after the radiation, the tumor came back and it was cancerous. Dad then pursued going to the University of Vanderbilt to see if there were any other options to fight this cancer. After the lengthy process, the doctors told him that they believed they could cure his cancer through an extensive surgical process. The surgery lasted over 14 hours, which consisted of three doctors working at the same time! Basically, they made an incision below his ear, down his neck to the front side of his neck, then up through the jawbone. The cancer tissue in his throat was removed and tissue was grafted from his arm to be used to totally rebuild the back of his throat. The surgery was difficult, but he never once complained.

His post care and rehab went well and it was about four months after the surgery that he was scheduled for a consult with the surgeons at Vanderbilt. After scans were completed and analyzed, the doctors confirmed that the cancer had invaded the other side of his neck! It was almost like the repeat of a bad dream. Daddy took the news well and conferred with the doctors about his options. Once again, surgery was scheduled and, as a family, we prepared to be there for daddy just like he had been there for us!

About six hours into the surgery, we were surprised to hear from the surgeon performing the surgery. He came out and informed us that the surgery had been stopped. Daddy's cancer had progressed and invaded the area that they had performed surgery on just months before. The cancer had wrapped itself around both arteries in his neck and there was nothing more anyone could do. The news was just devastating. It was like the air had been taken out of our bodies. How could I go on without my daddy? How could I make it?

Bill and Jessica, my brother's wife, drove down that evening to be with the family. I can remember my brother and me in the hotel room lying on the beds just crying! Daddy wasn't gone yet, but the news that the cancer was inoperative was just more than our emotions could take. The heartache we felt was beyond what mere words can convey. Already, loneliness set in. It was as if daddy had already gone, yet he was still here with a death sentence hanging over his head. All my brother and I could do was cry. Tears would come to a point where you just didn't think it was possible for any more to be left.

When dad first heard the news, I could tell it hit him hard. He was only in his mid-fifties and he just was not expecting that kind of news. God had already began to deal with my dad's heart and the heart that had been so kind and gentle to so many now was being softened toward God's invitation! While in the hospital room before his surgery, daddy had been watching a Billy Graham crusade on television. He would later tell mom the next day, that during the invitation, that God had spoken to his heart and he had prayed, asking Jesus into his heart and life. My daddy did not know it at the time, but God's salvation would become the rock that he would learn to cling to and it would provide the hope that he needed for the difficult fight ahead.

My dad was selected for a study that was being done through the University of Vanderbilt concerning experimental treatments for stage four cancers. He knew going in it was not going to be a cure. The treatments, at best, might offer a little more time with his family. Dad told Bill that he was willing to go through the treatments just to have a little more time to spend with those he loved. What he did not know was that God had another plan.

God used my daddy greatly in the remaining time he had. The spiritual part of my dad was growing and yearning to know more about his Lord. Bill or I would read the Bible to him on each visit at home. What a thrill it was for me to watch my daddy grow and bloom in the Lord! One special memory I have is a burden that God gave me at church. Bill, the pastor at our church, was serving the Lord's Supper and I began to think about how my dad had never known the blessing of Communion. So, I asked Bill if we could do that.......if we could have the Lord's Supper with my mom and dad at home. "No problem" was his answer.

By this time, my daddy had an airway in his neck because the upper part of his throat was obstructed by the growing cancer. Dad had a tracheotomy inserted to allow him to breathe, but he could no longer eat, he used a feeding tube. I thought, how are we going to do this? Then, as if the Lord just spoke to me, we'll just crush up the bread, put it into his feeding tube and we will pour the juice in the same way.

That night will forever be one of those blessings that God gives you for a keepsake treasure! You know the kind that is so special, so precious to you that you know in your heart that it will last till Jesus comes! God that night moved into my mom and dad's living room! His presence was so real! Such a sense of worship cannot be expressed with words.

Later on, as my daddy grew sicker with each passing day, I was reading Max Lucado's book, Traveling Light, about Psalm 23. I was reading the part dealing with death about how we have the grace we need for today, we have it today, but the grace we will need for tomorrow is not here yet. When tomorrow comes, it will be there! There had been so many times when the anxiety of losing my dad would just overwhelm me. I would think, when it comes time for Daddy to die, how am I going to get through it – how am I going to do it? After I read that, I thought okay, I am not there yet, but when I get there, God's grace will be there! I tried to remind myself of this truth every time fear would rise up within me about losing my dad. It has also been a great tool for me many times since my dad's passing. God gives us grace for our needs today, not for tomorrow. When tomorrow comes, the grace needed will be there! What a wonderful Savior we serve! How wonderful are His graces that we are blessed to experience every day!

I will never forget daddy asking Bill to preach his funeral. He was still in the hospital and had just learned that his cancer was inoperative. He would later ask our youngest daughter, Adena, while she was cleaning their house, to sing at his funeral. She was talented and it was certainly a God given gift. But this request would be her most special one! During Adena's teen years she was involved in her high school show choir, which sang and danced all over the country. Whenever they were local, mom and dad had always been there in the audience supporting her! How my daddy loved to hear her sing! But this time, it was Adena's time to support her mamw and papaw! When Daddy first asked her to sing at his funeral, it really took her off guard. She said, "Oh my!" Daddy said, "Do you think you can?" She said, "Papaw, I'll do it for you if you want me too!" He really wanted her to and even knew the song he wanted sung!

Daddy got to where he couldn't talk very plain. You could not understand him due to the tracheotomy in his neck. Bill gave him a bible and said, "Kyle, sometimes it just feels good to hold God's Word. There are times I just enjoy holding the Bible." This was a thin bible that Bill usually used at graveside services. Bill told daddy, "Sometimes just to hold it and know you've got God's Word in your arms." I can remember people coming and they would talk to Daddy and ask, "How are you doing, are things good with you and the Lord?" Even though he could not really talk to them and answer them, he would get that bible that he kept right on the end table and pick it up shake it at them and show it to them. That was his way of letting them know, yes, I am fine. He would do that and it was such a testimony; just picking up that bible and letting people see was a testimony.

Dad died on April 27th, 2002. His last week of life on this earth is one that will always be etched in my mind. Daddy couldn't talk and he kept pointing to the clock and then he would point up toward heaven. As he did so, he would hold up five fingers. We really didn't know what he was trying to tell us and it was a week later before the realization of what those five fingers meant. Daddy died five days from the day he pointed toward heaven and held up five fingers! Many of you may ask, "Do you think he knew he was going to go home in five days?" Yes, I do! I think God let my daddy know that he would soon be home and he was trying to prepare his family in the only way he knew how. The house was full of family and friends throughout that entire week. It seemed like one group would come and be there to support us and about the time they'd leave, another group would come in and take their place.

It was amazing to watch such a dying peace on my daddy that day. As bad as he was, yet he was still thinking of us. He patted me on the back showing me his love and the gentle care that I had always known from my dad. I will never forget the grace that God gave me all through daddy's sickness and I will never forget His grace that He gave to us as a family.

That Saturday, my daddy's sister-in-law had come to visit, who just happened to be a former nurse. As she and mom were talking my aunt noticed that daddy was beginning to slip away. Momma, Chad, Jessica, Adena, Bill and I stood around the bed and the rest of the family was right behind us. The room was filled with those that loved daddy and was there for his crossing. We each held hands around the bedside and Bill began to lead us in prayer. I watched daddy as Bill prayed and I witnessed my father take his last breath. Daddy always said amen at the end of prayer and I missed my daddy's amen at the end of Bill's prayer. But Bill said that Kyle had said amen this time on the other side of glory! We stood there for a long time saying our final goodbyes. Chad was crying so hard. I'll never forget, as Chad was leaning over his tears were falling on daddy's cheeks.

I did what I had told daddy I would do. I had told him you are not going to die, because Jesus has already done that for you. You are only going to go to sleep and you will wake in the most beautiful place ever and you will be with Jesus. I told him when the time comes that I'm not going to say goodbye. I am going to say the same thing I said to you at bedtime when I was just a little girl. I whispered in his ear, "Good night, daddy." Throughout the whole experience with daddy, from the beginning of the sickness to the end, I will never forget the hard times, the precious times, the sad times and the happy times! But more than anything, I will never forget God's most wonderful and most precious grace!

6

ANGELS UNAWARE

What we have once enjoyed and deeply loved,
we can never lose, for all that we love deeply
becomes a part of us.
—Helen Keller

In the many stages of my life I have experienced these words of Helen Keller. It seems tragic to once enjoy and deeply love, then to come to the place where we are separated by death. Our lives are changed, yet there remains so much connectedness with the past life.

I never cease to be amazed at the compassion and love of God. It truly mystifies me how God loves us even though we are sinners so undeserving of His love. He bestows His grace on us in ways which go beyond our acknowledgement. Such was the case with Buster, my dear little four-pawed Buddy! Buster came into my life at a time when God knew that I would need him; therefore, I believe Buster was sent to me as a messenger from God. This gift in my life reminds me of the verse in Hebrews: *Do not forget to show hospitality; in doing this, men have unsuspectingly entertained angels* (Hebrews 13:2 EDNT).

Some Bible students may jump on this thought, but they should remember that an "angel" is a messenger. Just read what I have to say before you rise in disagreement! Buster was a "messenger" to me!

Buster, a little mixed dog, came to us while my husband was off in graduate school in Oxford, England. My youngest daughter had been after me to get a dog, but we had a rather large, unruly dog in the past and that had not gone so well. So, I was apprehensive about getting another dog. My husband was totally against the idea. So, while he was away at school, we decided to go to the dog pound to check out those that were available for adoption.

When we entered the dog compound, the dogs were barking, jumping up and down; generally just excited at someone being there. At first I thought, "This is a bad idea." Then we noticed a little white fellow just standing in the pen not barking and not jumping up and down as if he were just waiting for us to come his way! It was as if he knew why we were there and he was thinking, "I am just what you need." As soon as we saw this little one year old guy, we just fell in love with him. He looked like a cross between a Maltese and a Poodle. He was small, looked undernourished and had big eyes that just seemed to grab your heart! When we inquired about him we were told his story. He had been adopted before by a young couple, but after taking him home, they found out their apartment building did not allow pets. So Buster was brought back to the dog pound in hopes of a new home. Needless to say, Buster was adopted and my husband was told while he was at the airport waiting on his plane back home. He was not thrilled about the idea, but after meeting Buster, he too fell in love with our little messenger.

Buster came into my life in 1998, just as my health was taking a turn for the worse. My diabetes was out of control and the doctors told me that it had gotten to a point where control was going to be hard to ever maintain. We had tried about everything, from adjusting my insulin to even trying an insulin pump. Still the diabetes remained out of control and the damage from long-term diabetes was taking a huge toll on my kidneys.

It was during this time my sugar levels would just abruptly drop, leaving me with such low sugars that I would be lifeless to the point of losing touch with reality. Once I was driving home from my doctor when my sugar level dropped to 19! I lost consciousness while driving by the local high school. The car was all over the road and was picking up speed. Directly ahead was the busiest intersection in town; two different roads, each having two lanes and I was heading straight for the intersection. From what I understand (I don't remember anything about that episode), I went right through the red-light and everyone else missed me! A few hundred yards away was the intersection of the mall and it was there that I would finally wreck!

The wreck was bad, very bad. There were four cars at the red-light waiting for the light to change. By the time my car hit the car in the back of the line, I was doing about 55 mph! My car hit with such force the first car was knocked into the next car; then that car was knocked into the next car, etc.

The front car at the red-light was hit with such force that it knocked the car through the intersection!

Right after the wreck my husband, who was visiting a friend in the hospital, came driving by and saw a long line of cars backed up due to the wreck. He said "something" just told him it was me. Sure enough, as he traveled around the line of cars through a back way, he saw the front of my car. It was all gone except for the front tag with my nick name, "Special Kay" on the front. He rushed to the car only to find me gone. He ran back to the ambulance and found me sitting up on the stretcher with the EMT's trying to get me to drink some orange juice with sugar added as they attempted to raise my sugar level. I was taken to the area hospital and treated for the low sugar level along with a scratch on my knee. All in all, the wreck had involved five cars and no one was hurt outside of my scratched knee! God is good! Is He not merciful and wonderful? His grace is always timely.

From that day until my first successful kidney transplant, I was unable to drive. You really do not realize how much driving you do as a wife, homemaker, mother, and grandmother until you cannot drive yourself any longer! This put a huge burden on my family; driving Miss Kay on all my errands was not a fun task. Maybe that is why some now say "walking with Miss Kay."

It also permitted me to spend quality time with God's little messenger! Buster and I became inseparable companions! He would sit in the recliner with me and we would spend the day together waiting for the rest of the family to get home. It was during this time that we really bonded;

unlike I had ever bonded with an animal before! Buster just became "my" dog! He did not really pay much attention to anyone else. We would walk together, I would talk to him and he would look back with those big brown eyes as if he understood every word.

Once I was very sick and confined to bed. My husband told me that he got up and took Buster out to do "his business." After returning to the house, my brother stopped by to check on me. While they were talking, Bill noticed that Buster was not where they were. He looked down the hall where my bedroom was and there was Buster waiting by the door wanting to be let back in the room to be with me! He was just sitting there looking toward where my husband was as if trying to tell him, "In there is where I want to be, now pay attention and let me in there. I have a job to do."

Buster was more like a little person than a dog. He brought such great comfort to me, not only when I was sick, but during the day when it was just the two of us. He would follow me from room to room as I went about my daily schedule. He would sit by my side as I spoke on the phone or at night when I would relax, he was always by my side. He truly was a "best friend" to me in so many ways. It was not words; it was his friendship, his unwavering love and the no pretense relationship we had with each other.

You have heard of "service" dogs, well Buster's life was a ministry to me. And this reminds me of a favorite scripture found in 2 Corinthians:

> 3. Praise God, even the Father of our Lord Jesus
> Christ, the Father of compassion, and the God

who stands beside you to encourage; 4. Who
stands beside us to encourage during any kind
of affliction that we in turn may be able to
encourage others every time afflictions arise,
by the consolation we received of God. 5. As
the sufferings of Christ overflows to us, our
consolation and encouragement flows from Christ.
(2 Corinthians 1:3-5 EDNT)

God is the God of comfort! He comforts us in all our troubles and tribulations. But He comforts us for more than just to bring comfort to our lives; He comforts us in preparing us to be utilized in His ministry of comfort to others. We are comforted and God takes that experience of comfort of His grace and uses it to impact another person's life that is going through a similar trial. We are able to connect with them due to our experience and they are able to connect with us! Personal suffering through a trying situation creates an opportunity to be an influence on behalf of Christ.

We do not normally think of trials, tribulations and suffering as an opportunity, but it is to the believer that allows the Holy Spirit to take personal experiences of grace and use them for His glory. These experiences can be used to encourage someone else in the faith. We can take those difficult times and let the Spirit use them to comfort someone else with that same comfort we received through the mercy of God.

I learned a lot of lessons from Buster. How much God loved me, or how He loved me enough to send me a little friend to comfort my bad days. There were those days when it was difficult to go on, yet it seemed as though God would just reach through Buster and encourage me! His big brown eyes that twinkled with such joy! His sitting on the couch with his paw leaning on the arm, just like a human would do just seemed to bring a smile to my face. His shameless love for me without regard as to what others thought also spoke to me. His unconditional love, his patience with me, his sacrifice to stay by my bedside while I was sick; there were so many lessons that God taught me through that little canine friend.

God has been my special friend (but He uses others, too), comforting me in all the challenges of my life. He has been by my side through difficult moments, never leaving me nor forsaking me. Those times when it seemed so difficult for me to keep going, my Heavenly Father was there using His resources to encourage me and support me, *"His eyes are upon the righteous and His ears are open unto their cry."* His everlasting love for me is without equal. God has been so loving, so tender and so patient with me. And the greatness of His sacrifice in sending His Son, Jesus Christ, to die on the Cross in my place; how could God love someone enough to make such a great sacrifice? I do not know, I just know He did!

God taught me much using my little friend! He taught me lessons of comfort and lessons of love. He taught me lessons of friendship and lessons of what it means to comfort someone while they are down. My God used one of His smallest canine angels to teach me many things and I will cling to those memories and those lessons learned at the altar of His love!

Helen Keller said it so well, *"Life is a succession of lessons which must be lived to be understood."* Life is about lessons; lessons of faith, lessons of comfort, lessons of love, lessons of hope, lessons of learning to help others and lessons about sacrifice!

This next quote also sums up what I am trying to express. Denise Klass said, *Death ends a life, but it does not end a relationship.* One day life on this earth will be done and when that day comes death will end physical life, but the relationships that we have made will not end. They will be lived out in those lives that we have influenced on behalf of Christ. They will be realized in the lives we have been blessed to touch. They will be lived out in the memories of all those that have watched God's grace unfolding in our lives. Death may end a physical existence on earth, but the relationships that have been born through adversary and comfort will continue!

7

SIFTED

The only way to learn strong faith
is to endure great trials.
—George Muller

31. And the Lord said, Simon, Simon, watch out,
Satan has desired to have you that he may sift
you as wheat: 32. But I have prayed for you, that
your faith fail not: and when you return to Me,
strengthen your brethren. (Luke 22:31, 32 EDNT)

Have you ever gone through such a difficult trial that
you actually could relate to Simon Peter in this text? Christ
informed him that Satan desired to sift him as one would sift
wheat, but that He had prayed for him not to fail. Christ, our
Great High Priest, being our advocate before the Father pleads
our case as Satan desires to sift us. That is what He was doing
for Simon Peter; He was interceding for him so that he would
not fail. Did Christ know that Peter would deny him three
times on the night that He was betrayed? Certainly He did!
But Christ was not just measuring the flesh; He was looking
at what His grace would accomplish in Peter's life! Jesus
understood Peter's human weakness, he also understood

Peter's value to the Kingdom and knew he would return to his firm stand and be able to strengthen others.

Such a year in my life was 1998. It was to be a year with incredible challenges and it would be a year that my emotions would become like a roller-coaster. Everything that went right also had a shadow to it that disrupted the blessings. For every answer to prayer, there was a new trial that would rise which had to be conquered before we could approach the next challenge. This was the year where it was determined that I needed to seek a transplant in order to live and maintain any quality in my life. Once the decision was made, with the help of Dr. Dan Carroll, my primary physician, we pursued a pancreas and kidney transplant. This, we discovered, was not a simple task. It was not just a matter of approaching the insurance provider and telling them, "I need a kidney and pancreas transplant so I can have some quality in my life." This transplant business is truly an involved ordeal that I would not wish on anyone!

The insurance company provided us with four different hospitals around the country that were on their list to perform this double surgery. From these, we would pick one. We chose the University of Maryland in Baltimore, Maryland. After traveling to meet the surgeons and transplant team, a whole series of tests had to be done before they could determine whether or not I was a viable candidate. Once that aspect was complete, we talked about donor possibilities.

My husband told them he wanted to be tested as a kidney donor (the pancreas would have to come from a cadaver). He was told they would test him, but he was not a "blood" relative, but a relative by marriage, so it would be nearly impossible for us to be a match. His remark back to them was, "Try me, you might be surprised." He was talking about the power of prayer. The power of God being unleashed in a situation and His glory is beheld. The tests were scheduled and we got a phone call about a week later informing us a miracle had happened. Bill and I had a kidney tissue match. The whole family and church family were thrilled! Everyone had been praying knowing Bill's desire to be my donor. This was one of those precious times in the Lord where you just witness God being God!

There is always a roadblock to the best plans. One of the tests was to make sure that there was no kidney damage or disease. These tests were vital to Bill being my donor. The test showed that his kidney was spilling protein and not functioning as it should. The probable cause was lupus, a disease that he had dealt with for over 10 years. Once again our hopes were dashed.

Bill talked to the medical staff and asked them to do another kidney test, but their response was there was no need. The test provided conclusive evidence that his kidney was spilling protein and that was that. Bill was persistent and would not accept that God was shutting this door. They finally agreed to do the test again. Bill and I went to the church family and asked them to pray and pray until they touched God on our behalf. The church prayed, our family prayed and fellow believers from other churches were praying as well.

Finally, the next week the test was completed a second time. The results were given the following week and not only

did the test show no protein spillage, the lupus disease did
not even show up as being positive. We rejoiced till there was
no energy left with which to celebrate. My husband was now
officially listed as my donor, but there were still other hills,
valleys and mountains to face.

We all face personal mountains, whether they are
connected to illness, family problems, financial troubles, or
other issues. It is not a question of whether we will have trials
and tribulations, for God revealed in His Word that every
believer would deal with tribulation all the days of their life.
The real mountain that we must deal with is how we are going
to respond to these monumental challenges.

Jesus explained to Simon Peter that Satan desired
to "sift him" as one would sift wheat. Satan wanted to grind
Simon Peter, to put him through so much anguish that he
would just fall apart. Have you ever felt that was happening in
your life? Have you ever been to a point where you felt your
life was coming apart and just breaking up? That is what Jesus
was telling Peter. Satan wanted to wreck him spiritually and to
destroy all that was valuable for the kingdom.

Satan still desires to sift believers. He desires to grind
us up, to sift us as a sieve would flour. By putting us through
his evil grinder, Satan tries to tear us apart and break down
our resistance. But remember, *"Greater is He that is within
you, than he that is in the world."*

At present, your life may be going through the sifter. It
may feel as if your life has been ground up till there is nothing
left for you, for others or for God. And that is just what Satan
wants for you to think. He is a master of deception. Satan

rejoices when we begin to doubt God or God's intention for our lives. He roars when he leads us to questioning God's purpose or desired will for us. Once we cross over into the realm of reasoning or rationalizing God's acts or action, then we have moved from the position of believing and trusting God to one of doubting and dishonoring God and His Word!

Philippians 3:10, *That I may know Him, and the power of His resurrection, and the fellowship of His sufferings, being made conformable unto His death.* Paul, basically in this verse, gave us his desired testimony. He wanted to know Christ, and he wanted to experience the power of Christ's resurrection, but there was an expectation for this to be known. He would have to suffer as Christ suffered in order to truly know the fullness of Christ's sufferings. Only then would he be made conformable in character to Christ's death.

When a believer truly suffers for the cause of Christ, there is a fellowship with Christ that will be experienced that cannot be known anywhere else. We understand far better the sufferings of Christ. We understand that Christ was poured out as a drink offering for the salvation of the world. And now we are being poured out as a drink offering for others. Why are we being sifted?

As we suffer in this life, our character can be changed into the image of the Savior. So that our character grows and we truly experience a closer relationship to Christ. We lean upon the Lord and He walks with us through every experience of suffering. He is there, fellowshipping with us through each adversity. In times of tribulation, we know Him in a way unlike any other experience. We witness the Savior suffering for us that He might be poured out as an offering to be experienced by all that desire to know Him in a more intimate way. It is in those experiences that our character is refined; refined into His likeness and into His image. The image of one giving Himself on behalf of others. He is dying that we might gain life. We suffer in order that others might see Him and know Him.

8

RETREAT

We are not retreating –
we are advancing in another direction.

—Douglas McArthur

Finally, after all the tests were completed and the transplant team had signed off giving their approval for the transplant, I was placed on the list and waiting for a pancreas. Within days, I received a package from the University of Maryland which contained a beeper. This beeper was to be carried with me at all times and once it went off, the clock would begin ticking for us to get to Maryland and check into the hospital. Time would be of the essence. Pancreas organs cannot last long outside the body, so we had to get to the hospital quickly, get prepped for surgery and then wait.

Late one Sunday evening, about the time Sunday night service was over, the beeper alarmed. I called the hospital and they informed me that a pancreas match had been found. We were to drive to Maryland as soon as possible. Bill was in route home from church when I called his cell. As I relayed the news, our energy level just seemed to explode. Thoughts were racing through both our minds! The hospital had prepped us for this process by teaching us to have a bag packed and ready to go ahead of time. I had accomplished that as soon as I had received the beeper and my name added to the transplant list. But when the actual message was given that the surgery was a go, it seemed as if there were a thousand things to do. I had to call certain family members to let them know that the surgery was now being scheduled. The anxiety levels were zooming and we did not have time to waste.

We contacted the church prayer line and the news spread like wildfire. We could tell the church family was praying. It is amazing how in the midst of so much commotion, there is this sense of God's peace and you just know that people are, at that moment, praying for you. It is comforting and also humbling. We had pursued a transplant, went through all sorts of tests, had disappointments and now it was finally happening.

It was a time of apprehension. The *"what if"* began to cloud our minds. What if we drive all the way there and it is a no go? What if we have this surgery and something goes wrong? What if something goes wrong with Bill's surgery.... how would I deal with that? On and on the "what if" thoughts would rush in, but all the while, God's Spirit was there comforting in ways that cannot be fully explained.

Now we had another problem, one not anticipated. Bill had been at the church almost all day. Sunday's for a Senior Pastor are long days and this certainly was no exception. Now he would have to come home, change clothes, pack our vehicle and drive nine hours to Baltimore and have surgery. The drive is a long one and with the anxiety surrounding us; it was one that God would have to watch over for us to make it to the hospital safe and sound.

Before we left home, daddy, mom, Bill, our youngest daughter, Adena, formed a circle, held hands and prayed (along with my best friend Buster of course). We prayed as a family trusting God for His will to be done in our lives and the life of our family. We also prayed for the family of the donor, which meant someone had just suffered the loss of a loved one.

Most do not realize what it means to be the recipient of an organ: there are many emotions associated with it, which are difficult to explain. Chief among the concerns is that another family has just suffered the loss of a loved one and in the midst of that loss, they donate the organs so that another family can save a life. You have mixed emotions: thrilled at the thought of getting your life back, but on the other side you realize that in attaining your dream, there are others who have just had their dream shattered. Gaining what had been lost for so long had to be weighed against another family's loss.

As I thought about what all this meant, it reminded me of our Lord and the greatness of His sacrifice! He gave up His life so my eternal life might be saved. He died that I might live. He did not have to give up His life, but He chose to do just that out of the greatness of His love.

As Bill continued to drive toward Maryland, with the new life for our family in front of us, those thoughts kept going through our mind. We continued to pray for the other family; for their loss and for the brokenness they must be experiencing. As the miles and hours passed by, one by one the riders in the car fell asleep. My mom was in the back seat and I was in the front. On a long stretch of interstate Bill finally dosed off himself. Thankfully, Bill woke up and turned the wheel as we approached a tractor trailer from the rear. It was as if the Lord had shaken Bill from his sleep and told him what to do. We passed the tractor-trailer in the left lane barely missing, traveling 70 M.P.H. Later in the morning, the same thing would happen a second time. This time, Bill fell asleep while passing a tractor-trailer and again he awoke just as our vehicle was about to go into the side of that huge truck! Surely a Guarding Angel was watching over us!

Have you thought about how many times God intervenes in order to take care of you? He is ever watching over us and He is constantly caring for us! His mercy and grace are always there for His children and, that night, down a long and tiresome stretch of interstate, we experienced that mercy and grace in a way that has never left me. May His name be praised for His wonderful works!

Arriving at the hospital in the early morning, first were the labs. They drew vials of blood and began prepping both of us for the pending surgeries. We were placed on the surgical floor; IV's were started and then began the process of the dreaded waiting. Waiting in those kinds of circumstances is hard. You just want to snap your fingers and make the process happen, but, that is not the reality of a major organ transplant. It is a slow, tedious, tiresome ordeal. We waited till early afternoon the word finally came....the surgeries were a no go!

They had cross matched my blood with that of the donor and it seemed a good match. More tests were showed my antigen levels had gone up meaning my body would instantly reject the pancreas organ. Staff explained that the particular antigen had been dormant in my system probably since the birth of my children. The antigens had shown in the first cross match. The surgery was cancelled and all of the effort was lost. At the end of the day, the only thing remaining was exhaustion, frustration, anxiety and a broke spirit. Of course, the question "Was this part of God's plan?" was obvious.

What is the source of your peace? Is it in your bank account or in your annual physical checkup? In all of our lives, situations can change so abruptly, so quickly, that it can totally take us off guard. What was not anticipated yesterday can become the reality today. Peace, that illusive positive force that is so fleeting at times; we all desire peace, but, from where does peace come? Isaiah stated that his "perfect peace" came from the Lord God of heaven! The question is "How do we attain it and how do we keep this perfect peace?"

First, we can attain God's peace only after we yield to His will. Second, Isaiah states that this peace is kept by the Lord; in other words, God is the granter of peace and He is the One that keeps us in peace. Perfect peace is not subject to circumstances; it is sustained by God and not by the issues of life. *You will keep in perfect peace him whose mind is steadfast, because he trusts in you* (Isaiah 26:3 NIV). Isaiah teaches us that "perfect peace" is maintained by the believer keeping his/her mind on God! Our minds are sustained by God and His Word.

God's Word reflects His promises that we are to believe and behave in the light of His grace. Have you ever witnessed a depressed believer when his or her mind is focused on the Lord? When our minds are focused on the Lord, the true greatness of His power and the greatness of His love are planted deep within our souls. Those seeds of peace are nurtured until we have perfect peace. Perfect means mature, as one would think of a teenager maturing and becoming a fully grown person. As we grow in grace and live in peace the spiritual lives mature. We learn to trust in a new and mature way. We learn through the experiences we have with God that He can and should be trusted!

> *Be careful (anxious) for nothing; but in everything by prayer and supplication with thanksgiving let your requests be made known unto God. And the peace of God, which passeth all understanding, shall keep (guard) your hearts and minds through Christ Jesus (Philippians 4:6-7).*

Paul wrote in the passage that we are to "be careful for nothing," which means do not worry about anything or be anxious about anything. As we draw near to the Lord, we are instructed to not worry or to have anxiety concerning the issues of our lives. Why? Worry and anxiety are not trusting in the Lord, but are the opposite of trust. We are to pray about everything and then put our trust in the Lord for His leadership and solution to the issue at hand. Connecting ourselves to God in praying over all the matters of life brings about a peace that is not of this world. It is a peace that is centered on giving control to God over our concerns in prayer and trusting Him to see us through all circumstances.

"The peace of God" refers to the believer being freed from fear, anxiety and worry that normally are associated with the deep concerns of our lives. God does not want us walking with fear (2 Timothy 1:7), but His desire is for us to seek Him out in all areas of our lives and then to lay those problems upon Him as an offering of trust and belief.

"Peace that passeth all understanding" means a peace that comes from God and that is given in times of anxiety. This peace is so wonderful, that it is beyond our capability to express or our capacity to understand. God's peace goes beyond the ability to understand problems. His peace leads to freedom from fear, a release from worry and a relief from anxiety. When God's peace is on-hand, we have nothing to worry about!

"Shall keep your hearts and minds through Christ Jesus" defines how Christ will guard believer's hearts and minds through the difficult issues of life. This is a military term which refers to a sentry standing on guard duty. His mission is clear: watch over that which is deemed valuable and stand fast that it might remain safe! Christ watches over us, His valuable Bride, and His mission is to keep our hearts (how we feel) and minds (how we think) in peace (not having fear)! That is what the Savior is doing for us as we present ourselves to Him in all the affairs of life!

*Character cannot be developed in ease and quiet.
Only through experience of trial and suffering can
the soul be strengthened, ambition inspired,
and success achieved.*
—Helen Keller

9

ABIDING

Success is not final, failure is not fatal:
it is the courage to continue that counts.
—Winston Churchill

4. Abide in Me, and I in you. As the branch cannot bear fruit from itself, except it abide in the vine; no more can you bear fruit, except you abide in Me. 5. I am the vine, you are the branches: He who abides in Me, and I in him, the same brings forth much fruit: for apart from Me you can do nothing. 6. If a man does not abide in Me, he is cast out of the vineyard as the unfruitful branch and is dried up; and they gather and burn them. 7. If you abide in Me, and My words abide in you, you ask what you will, and it will come to pass for you. 8. My Father was glorified in this, that you bear much fruit; and you shall become My disciples. 9. As the Father loved Me, so have I loved you: continue in My love. 10. If you keep My commandments, you shall abide in My love; even as I have kept My Father's commandments and abide in His love. 11. These things have I spoken that My joy might be in you, and that your joy may be fulfilled. (John 15:4-11 EDNT)

What does it mean to abide? It means to continue. But there are times that continuing on as a believer in the midst of a terrible storm seems impossible. But that is where abiding or continuing in Christ comes in to play. We abide in Him and He abides in us. *I am the vine, you are the branches: He who abides in Me, and I in him, the same brings forth much fruit: for apart from Me you can do nothing.* In the midst of our continuing, we are given the great privilege to see the true handiwork of His grace. I call this, "grace in action!" Only in the midst of testing, do we truly see God's real commitment to us.

It was most difficult to hear the words that the transplant surgery had been called off. Dealing with disappointment is such a difficult emotion. We all face it. We all have to endure these lessons in life, but disappointment is a reaction that carries a lot of baggage. The word disappoint means to fail to meet the expectations or hope of: frustrate, which means to induce feelings of discouragement. Frustration lends to the feelings of dissatisfaction that arises from problems being unresolved or needs being unfulfilled. That is a lot of emotion! But the disappointment and frustration that a person feels when they experience a loss is hard to express. It can certainly be characterized by the word discouragement and dissatisfaction. But with "whom" are we so discouraged or dissatisfied? That may be where the real battle is being fought!

For us, there was only one direction to go after the setback in Baltimore. We went home, back to the church family and we cried together and prayed together. Our church, during this time meant more to us than words can explain. New Life Baptist Church is a praying church. They do not just say they will pray for you, they do pray for you. Those prayers were the fuel that God used so many times to keep us going.

When we arrived home from this disappointing experience, there was our church with open arms and loving hearts caring for us as a mother would a hurt child. They were as deeply wounded by this disappointment as we were, but they kept their emotions in tact in order to minister to our family. So many times I have seen my husband, as the Senior Pastor, called to a needy family. They needed him to pray for them, to hold their hand during a tough trial or to give words of comfort in a dark period in their lives. But this time, we witnessed firsthand the church as a body of believers rising to meet the need of their shepherd's family. They were unbending in their faith, unwavering in their prayers and unconditional in their love for the entire family!

After getting our feet back on the ground and our faith refocused on the Lord rather than on our circumstances, we were once again ready to keep our eyes on the road ahead. That road would lead to another difficult curve. The hospital called about a procedure they wanted to try that would hopefully make a match a better possibility. Plasmapheresis (IVIG) treatment as it is often called is a process where the blood is removed from the system, the plasma part of the blood is removed and then the blood is returned to the person's system. By taking out the plasma of the blood, you also remove the antigens, which is what causes rejection. The doctor's thinking was that if we could lower the amount of antigens in my system, then the possibility of rejection would be lessened.

Arrangements were made for us to return to the University of Maryland hospital to begin the treatments. The insurance company provided a place to stay and Bill, my mom and I began the long process that would prayerfully lead us toward a successful transplant. Every day I would go to the hospital to have my IVIG treatment and then every couple of days they would take my antibody count. This process would be continued for two weeks (that is as long as you can separate plasma and blood). After two weeks of treatments, they would cross match my blood with that of another person's to see if we were a good match. The treatments lowered my antigen levels to a point where a successful transplant was much more likely. Now, all we could do is wait.

We had to wait till my blood matched another donor's blood. Sadly, that also meant that we were waiting for someone to have an accident or to die of some illness. That is dealing with a difficult emotion. What is most difficult about a cadaver donor is that while you are praying for an organ to be found, it means that someone will die for you to receive an organ; another family is praying that their loved one will live. My emotions were continually at odds with this contradiction. Certainly, I wanted a transplant so I could live and have some sort of normal, healthy life, but the other side of me did not want a family to endure that kind of loss. I knew for me to live meant some loved one would have to die. This is one area where God's grace would have to intervene on my behalf.

On April 6th, the day of my brother's birthday, the hospital called and informed us that they had an organ on the way and we were a match. Instantly everything went into motion at our hotel room. We scrambled to get ready, making phone calls to family and friends and hurriedly tried to get to the hospital. As soon as we arrived, the hospital staff began to prep me for surgery. The hospital received the organ and immediately began testing it to make sure everything was a go. As I thought about the soon coming transplant, I thought about how great it would be for me to receive my transplant on Chad's birthday*!

---

*Chad, Miss Kay's younger brother, shares his thoughts about his sister.

Kay is a really good person. She has such a good heart. We have always been really close, even though we are 15 years apart in age. We always got along really well. I have always admired her being able to do all she does while still being sick. Her faith is remarkable. I don't know anyone who would have everything...not just diabetes and kidney failure, but everything in the book, and she keeps a positive attitude. It is hard to see someone you love suffer so much and have so many disappointments. Kay has been through so much, but her faith is much stronger than mine. She has more optimism than anybody I know. Kay never gets upset or angry. She just takes it in stride. She is tough - tougher than I am! —**Chad**

What appeared to be a "go" on Chad's birthday ended up being a "no-go" before the surgery. The hospital that retrieved the organ had damaged it. The staff at Maryland could not risk doing the transplant with a damaged organ that most likely would not be viable. We left to deal with our emotions and to return to treatment. Again, another heart break and another failed opportunity.

But one thing you find out as you walk this journey called life. When you walk with God, and things go wrong, it does not mean it is over. Nothing is impossible with God! How many times we quote that verse and yet we were about to learn that "not now" does not mean "never!" When God closes one door, He opens another.   On April 8, 1999, I was in IVIG treatment when Jessica, my transplant coordinator, came with happy news that another organ had been found. A cross match had shown that we were a match and the organ was in flight. The entire room broke out in applause. Everyone was so excited. Once again, calls were made, family informed and people were alerted to pray.

They sent me and Bill down to pre-op to begin the task of getting ready for surgery. We were in a holding room together and I remember looking over at him and thinking, "I'm about to get his kidney!" We talked, we prayed and this was such a special moment in our lives! What we had worked so long for was about to happen. They took us down to the operating rooms, Bill's right beside of mine! Two surgical teams would take part in the surgery. One to retrieve Bill's kidney and the other would do my transplants. They began Bill's surgery first and every few minutes a member of my team would give me an update on how Bill's surgery was going. Then, suddenly, there was his kidney; the pancreas was already there in a bowl of ice waiting. The surgeon asked me if I wanted to see my new pancreas. I said, "Sure!" He held it up and that is one of the last things I remember before going to sleep. The transplant was successful and so was Bill's surgery. I have no idea how long I was unconscious and the only time they allowed me to be conscious was when they wanted to let me know what was happening.

A few hours after the transplant, I developed complications. The pancreas was rejecting and forming clots in the blood vessels, which essentially killed the organ. What started out so positive and looked so promising was now hopelessly lost. During the time the pancreas was rejecting, Bill was also having problems due to an allergic reaction to the after-surgery medications. He felt like something was stuck in his throat and it became hard to breathe so he contacted the nurse concerning the choking. The response was that everything was fine, but the choking was getting worse. Once again, he called the nurse and once he saw the situation, other nurses were called for assistance. This became a crisis situation by this time, Bill had little respiration and his airway was almost closed. The floor nurse took command and immediately asked if anyone had taken time to look in his throat. Bill shook his head and the nurse proceeded to evaluate his throat.

The medication had caused the small lobe in the middle of Bill's throat to swell and block his airway. The *uvula* had swollen so much that the tip of it was pressing against his front teeth. After emergency medications were given, the *uvula* began to reduce in size. It was during this time that Bill found out about my medical situation. Twelve hours after my surgery, mom shared that I had lost the new pancreas. Bill knew something was terribly wrong, just by the look on her face. All that we had worked for so long had now been for naught. His heart was crushed and he later shared with the church the following months were some of the darkest spiritual times he would ever endure.

Mom was told that all was well after the transplant and that she should get some rest. Right after returning to the room, the phone rang and the doctor informed her of my complications. Returning to the hospital, she learned about the loss of the pancreas. She was devastated. How could all that had gone so well now go wrong? I was in trouble with the new pancreas and Bill was having an allergic reaction, but mom was there alone!

The rejection of the pancreas caused the new kidney to go into acute rejection. With this sudden onset with the kidney, we were fighting a battle on every front. Not only had I lost the new pancreas, now I was in jeopardy of losing my transplanted kidney. Emergency 12-hour surgery was required to take out the rejected pancreas. Once again my body was subjected to the trauma of additional surgery. The situation was getting worse.

Due to the acute rejection with the new kidney, the doctors placed me on stronger anti-rejection medications. On top of that, my body was showing signs of infection. The doctors were trying feverishly to save my kidney, but they had multiple battles to fight. Two days later, they had to operate on me again. This time they were trying to flush and cleanse my system of the bacteria and germs that were causing the problems. This would be my third surgery in 48 hours. My body was struggling while the doctors were trying to save the transplanted organ.

Now Bill was doing better with his allergic reaction and was brought in a wheelchair to my bedside. He was shocked at my appearance: there were ten different IV lines going into my body pumping me full of medications. They had two central ports going into my neck, each side of my neck could take three more IV lines and both arms had IV lines. Bill was shocked at how fast things changed. We had gone from talking to each other in pre-op to me fighting to hang on to life! No books that can adequately instruct anyone in such matters: only personal experience with God is sufficient. As believers, there are those lessons that can only be learned in the heat of battle. God was teaching us some hard lessons about living, about faith and about His work of grace!

Grace for most believers is connected to God's favor, so we do not normally associate it with suffering in the sense that it is God's grace to teach us something through suffering. We typically think of God's grace as His power being utilized to bring us out of a storm or difficult situation, but God's grace can and is used to teach us lessons in the midst of the fire. For most of us, these are lessons we had soon not learn. However, God's grace is designed to develop, strengthen, mature, and teach us the great truths of God's Word.

God's grace is designed to mold us into the image of His Son! This molding process is not always easy. Over the next few months we learned this the hard way. The process is on-going every day of our lives. With each trial, each storm, each testing of our faith, God's grace is given to teach us trust, to learn faith and to develop dependence on Him. It is also used to validate that God is exactly as He is described to be in His Word.........God is faithful and true!

Have you ever thought that the devil must surely be rejoicing over some mishap you experienced as a believer? When you stumbled into sin and brought reproach on God's Name? Have you ever pictured Satan just celebrating over your sorrows? During such times, these words in Micah have meant so much to me!

> *"Therefore I will look unto the Lord; I will wait for the God of my salvation: my God will hear me. Rejoice not against me, O mine enemy: when I fall, I shall arise; when I sit in darkness, the Lord shall be a light unto me" (Micah 7:7-8).*

Notice what Micah is saying concerning the difficulties of his life. He did not say we would "not fall," but ..."when I fall". He is stating the obvious, that believers fall and have their moments of suffering and hardships just as everyone else. But Micah goes on to teach us what he learned through those falls; he will arise! Out of those ashes of misery, out of the gloom of despair, and out of heartache and heartbreak he would arise! That is the deeper message that God teaches through Micah.

God is faithful and His grace is far reaching. His grace is not limited by situations or by our lack of strength. When our strength has ended and when our storm has reached the point that all earthly hope is lost, then His grace can and will rise to the occasion to free us and help us to prevail over ourselves and over the situation. That is not to say that our set of circumstances will change drastically, they may well remain

the same. That does not mean that our suffering will be less
severe or what caused the heartbreak will completely change.
What it does mean is that in the midst of it all, God will be
there, give His grace in those times of great need and teach us
patience! Just look at what Paul learned during his troubles.
His words explain this concept well:

> 3. And not only, but we also glory in hardships
> and sufferings: because we know that troubles
> produce patient endurance; 4. and patient
> endurance approves character; and character
> brings hope: 5. and a faithful trust in God's
> promises will never put us to shame; because
> the love which God has for us is poured out in
> abundance in our hearts by the Holy Spirit which is
> God's gift (Romans 5:3-5 EDNT).

Think of the magnitude of what those words are saying
to us! Tribulation or the trials in our lives are developing
patience and producing perseverance - the perseverance we
will need as we continue on this life-long journey that God
has planned for us. Perseverance produces experience or
character. What kind of character? Godly character, the kind
revealed through the life of Christ! Our character will become
more like His character! Our mannerisms will be more like His.
Our responses will be more in tune with Christ' responses.
We will think as He thinks, we will act as He acts and we will
respond as He would respond. The Word confirms this concept
of our behavior.

> Let this mind be in you, which was also in
> Christ Jesus: (Philippians 2:5 KJV). Also, Let our
> disposition and thoughts be the same as Christ
> Jesus: (Philippians 2:5 EDNT)

That experience or character will then produce hope! Character produces hope or faith based on the promises of God. This hope is not something based on a wish or an uncertainty, but on the unchanging promises of God! Character builds within us a faith that sees God and His promises for what they are: unchanging, undeniable and unaffected by circumstance! And this hope produces within us an attitude of believing God when our circumstances may indicate just the opposite.

Circumstances may appear that no one could change them, but faith leads us to take God at His word rather than accepting the circumstance. Hope that is based on the promises of God is faith in action. This is not faith based on human sight, but faith built on thus saith the Word of God! Corrie ten Boom's words serve as a good reminder of how believers should handle times of difficulty.

> *Look around you and you'll be distressed; look within yourself and you'll be depressed; look at Jesus, and you'll be at rest!*

We should never take our eyes off the Savior! Hebrews 12:2 "Looking unto Jesus the author (originator) and finisher (perfector) of our faith..." It is God that has been the originator of our faith, He has given us the seed of faith to believe in Jesus Christ His Son and it is He that perfects or matures our faith. God never intended for our faith to begin then remain there in its original state. His plan is one of growing our faith or expanding our faith, not by what our human eyes, but by our heavenly eyes that are focused on what God has said. Go back to the verse at the beginning of this chapter:

*I am the vine, you are the branches: He who
abides in Me, and I in him, the same brings forth
much fruit: for apart from Me you can do nothing.
(John 15:5)*

Without Christ you can do nothing.......as we face our
trials we begin to realize just how limited we are in this human
body. We begin to realize that the majority of life is not in
our own control, but is being controlled by forces outside
ourselves. Our health may take a turn that has nothing to do
with decisions that we have made or we may lose our job due
to a layoff, which we did not cause.

The real part that we play and the direction our life
takes is in the decision making process. When our health takes
a downturn, how do we respond? If we get laid off from our
job, how do we respond to the news? On and on life's issue
come at us and the only real means of shaping our lives is how
we respond. Do we turn to the Lord in these times or do we
simply try to work it out ourselves? Do we respond in faith to
these challenges or do we become depressed and despair over
the circumstances? Do we trust God in whatever we are facing
or do we turn on Him to falsely blame Him?

We are to abide in Him! Remember, abide means to
continue! We are to continue in Christ and to continue to walk
by His Word and in His Word! We will have realities to face
in many storms but those realities are not the final authority
concerning the difficulties. Jesus said to the storm, *"Peace,
be still."* In our trials He has the power to do that, but we
have to realize that He may choose not to still the storm. The
storm may be the conduit to the advancement of our faith

and the development of our hope! Character built out of experiences with God is character that is seasoned with grace! And that grace will help us to continue. Not to give up, but to continue. Continue in what we know is truth and reject what is untruth! If we abide in Him and He abides in us, then we are to continue to follow Him with eyes fixed and focused on His guidance and not our own!

10

THE VALLEY OF THE SHADOW OF DEATH

Faith is the strength by which a shattered world shall emerge into the light.
—Helen Keller

4. Yea, though I walk through the valley of the shadow of death, I will fear no evil: for thou art with me; thy rod and thy staff they comfort me. 5 Thou preparest a table before me in the presence of mine enemies: thou anointest my head with oil; my cup runneth over. 6 Surely goodness and mercy shall follow me all the days of my life: and I will dwell in the house of the Lord forever. (Psalms 23:4-6)

Valleys are dark because of one reason: the absence of light! My valley was a dark one at this time. I had just lost the pancreas and now my newly transplanted kidney was in jeopardy and in danger of rejection. Within a few days of my first transplant surgery, I now had to endure two more surgeries. The first was to take out the failed pancreas and the second was trying to cleanse the site that had developed infection. My condition grew worse by the day.

The anti-genes that had fought to kill my new pancreas now turned on my transplanted kidney with a vengeance! My body recognized my new pancreas as a foreign object, like infection, and it formed anti-genes to fight it off, much like the body forms anti-genes to fight off infection. Once the pancreas fight was over, my immune system now turned its focus on my new kidney. In the middle of all this battle was my life, or what was left of it. What started out to be a cure for my diabetes and kidney disease had now turned into a fight for my life! No longer were my sugar levels the most important health issue, now it was just keeping me alive long enough for my body to respond.

The darkness of this valley was first entered by my husband. Bill walked into this dark valley depressed and feeling abandoned! We had gone from being so excited about me getting a pancreas/kidney transplant to wondering each day whether I would survive. He stated that the kind of battle that we had entered was most difficult because he felt helpless. All the years that we had worked on fulfilling our dream of me being free of diabetes was now a distant memory. Now we faced a much bigger fight; the fight to keep me alive.

In Psalms 73, there is an interesting picture. The writer is faced with the dissolution of life's hard trials. In verse 1, he states that God has been good to Israel, the nation, but in verse 2: he states that as for himself, his feet had almost stumbled meaning that he was stumbling in his walk with God. Verse 3 gives an overview of his reasoning into this. He had become envious of the foolish because of their prosperity.

They had everything the heart could wish for and he as a believer was only persecuted day after day!

Have you ever felt like that? Have you ever looked at the life of a lost person and not felt jealousy at their prosperity? That is where my husband was at that moment. He had been through many trials as a believer and had been in the hard battle for a long time. He was tired of all the spiritual warfare that we both had been through. This would be the challenge of our spiritual lives! Spiritual warfare is a systematic battle in which the devil brings battles our way that are specially designed to bring the most damage and hurt possible. It is through this plan that he inserts himself into our lives and projects his will against ours and that of the Heavenly Father.

Satan's battle plan has two fronts as we see in Ephesians 6:16 "Above all, taking the shield of faith, wherewith ye shall be able to quench all the fiery darts of the wicked (wicked one)." Notice the writer uses the word "quench" in this text which means to put out. Believers are to put out the fiery darts that are sent against them. These darts have a two-fold purpose: (1) they are darts (arrows) that have a designated target – the devil knows our weak areas and he targets those areas for attack (2) they are darts that are on fire, which means after the arrow has hit its desired target he intends for the damage to spread!

In such a spiritual battle, the devil approaches the battle with his two-fold plan in mind. He targets our weak areas and then spreads the damage to other areas of our spiritual life! His plan has been tried and tested over many years of working against God's children. If Satan can divide us, then he can conquer us! When our allegiance is split away from the Father, Satan can defeat us and strip us of spiritual joy and our spiritual goals. *A double-minded man is unstable in all his ways.* (James 1:8)

A double-minded person is unreliable. When our faith is divided, we are torn between believing (taking God as His word) or in believing what we see or think. Being double-minded in this world is easy. All one needs to do is put their mind on the circumstances and stop thinking and they will receive no help to weather the storm. Satan loves to separate us from our faith. Not salvation faith, but daily, living faith. The kind of faith works to keep us from falling and not responding to the Holy Spirit's leadership. Faith that is active in protecting us, guiding us and leading us, is living faith. Is your life under attack, undergoing assault after assault and becoming divided in your allegiance? That is part of Satan's warfare against believers. He will attack when we are off guard; he will seek to divide us and then leave our lives shredded and in despair.

Is your strength emerging into the light? If it is, then it is your faith that is strengthening you and Christ, who is pouring Himself into you! Rest assured Jesus is there in ever trial that we face! He has promised to never leave us or forsake us. Whatever storm you are now facing or going through, remember, God is with you and for you in every step of the journey.

11

WHY?

There is no pit so deep but that His love is deeper still.
—Corrie ten Boom

Mom and my husband really dreaded telling me what
had happened. They had watched me fighting to keep the
pancreas, then losing it and now fighting for my life! What
would be the effect of their news on my resolve to go on?
How would it impact my emotional state? How would I deal
with the news? When I became alert enough, they explained
fully what had happened! I'm not sure what it was; but God
just watched over me and took care of me. I took the news, all
of it, just fine! I didn't get upset; I just had a spiritual calm on
me that was truly a peace that passes all understanding! It is
strange I know, but there are times in our spiritual lives that
God just divinely takes over and this was one of those times!
God just blessed me with peace and a calm spirit! Not a hope
so peace, where inside we are thinking, *"Ok, now God is going
to do this miracle in my life and heal my pancreas!"* It was
more like a comfort where you are under His authority and His
divine protection.

The following weeks would just be more trials as I was weaned off the ventilator. They had to make sure I could swallow without choking before going back on solid foods. We also had to now learn how to deal with my diabetes and deal with anti-rejection drugs at the same time! That could create real problems once I went home!

I came to the University of Maryland with such great hopes of leaving without diabetes, without needles, without the need for insulin and without the attending complications of diabetes. But in reality, my physical state leaving the hospital was worse than when I arrived. Now I had my immune system suppressed, no way to fight off infection and I still had diabetes. How could things have gone so wrong? "Why" was my husband's daily question.

Why is one of the most humanistic responses that we ever have, and it seems to be against a believer's faith that permits the Word to infiltrate our minds. We have been taught to just trust and obey...don't ask questions that would be distrustful of God's Word. Well, that may spin well from the pulpit, but it does not do much in the reality of life! Believers live in the real world that is full of trouble, sorrows and pain, but we are told not to ever ask why. This just does not seem to be a good fit to me. After all, if we do not ask "why," will we ever learn from the bad experiences in our lives?

My husband once preached a message on the subject "Why." It was a message that was borne in the midst of suffering, pain and questions. He shared that we need to change the why question. First, we need to re-look at the word to find new meaning. He used an acrostic of the word,

WHY, to teach us a quick way to address this issue. He stated, "God has taught me when the storm rages to look at the issues that surround it - think of the **"W"** as referring to **what.** What is it that you are trying to teach me through this storm? What is it that you want me to see spiritually through these circumstances? What is it that I need to learn so that I can grow and improve my spiritual walk? Instead of "why", ask **what**!

Then move to the second letter in why and let the **"H"** stands for **hindrances**. What hindrances are in my life that are keeping me from improving as a believer? What hindrances or besetting sins are slowing down my spiritual growth? What is hindering me from running the human and spiritual race well? What is hindering the areas of my life that God wants me to change? Hindrances just bog us down in the things of this world and weigh on us till we are no longer running the race of faith; we are barely walking! God may be using this storm to reveal the hindrances that are in the way of His grace working in your life.

The next letter is **"Y"** and it stands for **yield.** When we are able to see clearly "what" God is teaching us through the difficulties we can see what is hindering His work of grace in our lives. Now, we are ready for God to challenge our obedience or our readiness to yield and say, "Yes, to your will and your way!"

In the Old Testament story of Joseph, his life was one storm after another. His brothers sold him into slavery, and then told his father that he was killed by wild beasts. His employer's wife accused him falsely and he was imprisoned.

Even his fellow inmate would forget him even though he had interpreted a dream which foretold his soon coming freedom! Later after Joseph was freed from prison and appointed second only to Pharaoh, did he begin to understand God's "why" in his life. As his brothers would come to Egypt to buy food their family so desperately needed, God's lessons became clear as to what God had been doing in Joseph's life.

What were the lessons that God taught Joseph? Even though his brothers meant what they did for evil, God meant it for good! Through the sin and circumstances associated with it, God used the process to save His people from the coming famine. Joseph learned at every turn there were hindrances to God's will and plan, but that God was always working for his good and for God's glory! Joseph also learned how to peaceably yield himself to God and not exalt himself against God's plan, no matter what the cost!

Have you learned the powerful way of asking questions about your circumstances? What is God teaching you about yourself? Have you learned that God has a plan for your life? What "hindrances" are in the way of God from taking you to the next step in your journey of faith? Are you ready to yield everything to Christ? When one can come to this place in life, then the Savior can stand in front of the storm and declare, "Peace, be still" interpreted, "enough...silence!"

12

GRIEF EXALTED

For I consider the sufferings we now endure not worthy to be compared with the glory about to be revealed in us.
—Saint Paul

The highest honor that God can confer upon His children is the blood-red crown of martyrdom. The jewels of a Christian are his afflictions. The regalia of the kings that God has made are their troubles, their sorrows, and their grief(s). Grief exalts us, and troubles lift us.
—Charles Spurgeon

We had been in the hospital about two weeks and my surgeries were finally healing. Everything seemed to be going better until the next valley. During this entire time, I had been on a ventilator and when they removed it, the tube had caused a lot of swelling. The swelling caused me not to swallow correctly and my food would try to go down the wrong way. So, I could not eat or drink anything without a feeding tube. I could only whisper and needed voice therapists to regain throat function to eat and drink. Each day we had hope that this would be the day that I could swallow, but each day just dragged along and one day was just like the one before.

Finally, a swallowing test showed enough healing to start eating. They would schedule different foods with different consistencies and as I was able to swallow one food group they would start another one. That was the process until we finally was able to move to liquids. Liquids were the big test. Once I passed that test, they told me I was ready to go upstairs and eat and drink! It is amazing how many things we take for granted: like eating and drinking. What a happy day, after three weeks I passed my swallowing test. During those days I took new medications, over 20 pills every morning and then more pills three more times a day There were anti-rejection drugs to keep me from rejecting the new kidney and other drugs to keep other reactions down.

What began as a journey to get a new pancreas and be free of diabetes was now one of still having diabetes and taking all kinds of meds to keep the transplanted kidney from rejecting. To compound matters, my immune system was suppressed, and I was subject to about any virus, cold, flu or anything else going around. I had to learn to be so careful; no longer could I afford to take my health for granted. If the wrong virus entered my body, it could spell rejection of my transplanted organ and a lot of sick days. Finally, the doctor decided I was well enough to be released. We stayed that night and prepared for the long trip home.

Looking back over the weeks in ICU, the long ordeal was a nightmare! Because I tried to pull out the ten IV lines, they strapped me down so that I would not harm myself. I remember waking up from a drug induced coma and realizing I was strapped to the bed. Every time I woke up I was frustrated with those straps.

The nights always seemed fearful and long. Mom and Bill leaving for the night was a problem. I could hardly wait to see their face the next morning. During the day I could feel their presence and knew I was OK. Knowing they were there, even if I were asleep, I could just feel their presence. No matter what the doctors said, there are still times when only God can take away those fears, so I learned to lean on Him and His presence at night. This was an important time of spiritual growth for me knowing that God was there with me. At night I would feel so alone and then God whispered, "I am here. I didn't leave you. I'm right here with you!" I really began to feel His presence and knew in my heart that He was the One calming my fears. As Charles Spurgeon said:

....*The jewels of a Christian are his afflictions....*

The beginning of this chapter deals with the issue of suffering and how God uses that suffering to refine us. "Grief exalts us" was a strange twist of words for me. When I think of grief, it is loss or some cause of suffering that is caused by a significant event. As I look back on this experience, I realize that each of us were grieving in our own way and trying to come to terms with an unexpected loss. For my family, they were grieving the loss of a new life for me. They had envisioned me getting a new pancreas and being diabetes free. The new kidney would mean no dialysis in my future, so they focused on their loved one having a new lifestyle and a new future without all the ill effects of disease. This was a natural expectation.

For my husband, he too had envisioned all this and more. He would gain his soul mate back! Our relationship had become one of him being a caregiver and of me trying to survive. We had come to a point where we did not know what a normal day was. So he foresaw a day when our lives would return to what they had been in the past. Loving, caring, sharing, spending quality time together while being able to enjoy life together rather than constantly worrying about the next moment. He also envisioned a day when I would be able to be the complete mom to our daughters that I had been before the normal results of diabetes began to impact the family.

For me, I not only experienced the loss of my own dreams but I also had to understand the loss my family was facing. This was the most difficult aspect of my grief. Grieving for ourselves is one thing, but when you compound that with feeling empathy for others, that is more difficult. The pain my family was experiencing was serious and there was nothing I could do to relieve their pain. My loss then was two-fold. I grieved for my personal loss and my dreams of a new life free from diabetes and dialysis. And the grief my family was suffering compounded my feeling of desperation. The big question in my mind, "Had I let my family down?" I knew that I had not, but at times it sure felt that way.

Have you ever had a loss and you felt responsible, even though you knew it was not your fault? It is during these times, when believers open their heart to the Holy Spirit, that they learn valuable lessons. The Bible states clearly that we comfort others with the comfort we have experienced ourselves. God uses the times of suffering to comfort us, demonstrate His faithfulness, and to confirm that He is Faithful and True! He promised not to leave nor forsake us, and during these times, He confirms His Word.

The fact that grief exalts and troubles lift us, can benefit our lives if we allow God's Spirit to complete His work. That does not mean that we will understand everything God is doing right away. Some lessons are learned a little at a time. Others are learned as they are placed one upon another. But God has a work that He is working in each of our lives. Sometimes that work is hidden in His grace as He matures us and develops within us His character.

I learned many lessons of faith while grieving the rejection of precious transplants. Suffering through cycles of pain and disappointment, depressions and fears, showed me that God used my grief to build personal character and spiritual strength. By that, I do not mean that His intention was to make me more important, but to raise me up in character and spiritual standing by making me more distinctive as an individual Christian. God sought to bring positive change in all aspects of my life. This should be the goal of each believer. What if God determines the only way for us to be more like Him is through suffering?

Paul inscribed these words in scripture and I believe they are the words of every believer's heart - to know Christ in a personal and intimate relationship:

*That I may know Him, and the power of His
resurrection, and the fellowship of His sufferings,
being made conformable unto His death.
(Philippians 3:10)*

To know the power of His resurrection so that when temptation comes, we will know by experience the power of God, which leads us to be overcomers. To fellowship with the Savior in His sufferings should be an honor. As we suffer in this life, we realize more about His suffering on behalf of the human race and the great price He paid to save those who believe! Then, the end product of all this is to be made more like Him in personal behavior and lifestyle in front of others and how we represent Christ to a lost world. Does grief elevate us spiritually? Yes, if we yield ourselves to God and allow Him to complete His work in our lives. As I look back, I learned much through my loss and what I gained was what I really needed. A quote from one of the missionaries killed by the Auca Indians in Peru, speaks to this issue:

*He is no fool who gives up what he cannot keep to
gain that which he cannot lose.*

—Jim Elliot

13

DETOURS

Worry does not empty tomorrow of its sorrow,
it empties today of its strength.
The jewels of a Christian are his affliction.
—Corrie ten Boom

Have you ever had life throw a big detour sign in front of you? You were traveling down life's highway and everything seemed to be fine, then all of a sudden, you see a detour sign! This detour sign takes you off the road and side tracks your journey. Such was our case; everything seemed to be going in a certain direction in my life. Then, the detour sign and off we went on a new course and a new direction. But that doesn't mean that God had changed the destination, but how He wanted us to get there!

Home after my transplant surgery, life became more difficult. I kept wondering, when am I going to feel better? After three months had passed my transplant coordinator told me, "It's just going to take time." I just felt bad all the time and was not up to par mentally, physically or spiritually. The daily grind of being a transplant patient was not what I had expected. We had to have labs drawn weekly, doctor visits were just about every day and taking all the meds was an experience I would not wish on anyone! Through it all, my life slowly began to get back to normal. I had already decided not to try for another pancreas transplant, but did not realize that this sent shock waves through the family. By resisting another pancreas transplant, I was telling my husband I would just put up with dialysis until it killed me.

Bill stated that my decision not to have a transplant was the darkest time of his life. He was trying to hang on spiritually to his faith and pray that God would perform a miracle without another transplant. He knew that God had the power to heal, but he also knew that many had prayed for healing without a transplant and God's answer had been "Not that way!" Bill came to believe that we had taken a huge detour and became doubtful that we would find our way back to the right path he envisioned us to walk.

It was about a year later that I started thinking about the whole ordeal, a little at a time; nothing dramatic, but the thought just hit me, "I'm going to do this again!" Then the transplant center from the University of Maryland called and said my name was still on the transplant list, but it was inactive. They asked if I wanted to be on the active list and be considered for another pancreas transplant. I asked for a little time and began to pray about the matter, and talk with my family. We all came to the conclusion that it was time to try for another pancreas transplant! We contacted Maryland and I was activated on the list for possible donors. Within a week, the hospital called that they had a donor pancreas and I was a match!

We did not even have a beeper! They also said there was no time to drive; we would have to fly to Baltimore to meet the time deadlines. I called the family, mom couldn't go, but Adena, my youngest daughter, went even though she was pregnant with her first child. Baltimore said that no helicopter was available so we had to rush to the local airport. They were holding the plane, amazing there were exactly three seats left for us. Isn't God great?

Arriving at the hospital, the doctors were rushing to do lab work, start IV's, check my sugar levels, etc., but the surgery room waiting on us. The longer a donor organ stays out of a body the more chances there are of rejection or other complications! So my doctors were all business concerning getting me on the table and getting this procedure done!

What was so amazing concerning all this was the peace that I had once the decision was made to try for another transplant. God's peace just seemed to be so real and timely. It just seemed as if God had wrapped His arms around me, comforting me through the entire process and the surgery was a success, even though they used strong drugs to counter infection and had to watch my fluctuating enzyme levels! Admitted to the hospital on March 21 and discharged on April 7.

Even though I was discharged from the hospital, I would still have to go to the hospital for daily lab work, etc. Mom was flying to Baltimore so Bill could return to work. We had one day to get mom up to speed before Bill left. Little did we know that our plans would be totally changed!

We picked up mom from the airport and after getting her settled in the hotel, Bill received a call from a transplant nurse who requested that I return to the hospital and be readmitted. She stated that my lab numbers had risen sharply and we could be facing some problems. Bill asked her what the numbers were and she did not have the numbers. Bill believed it was a mistake. He had received a detailed list my lab numbers daily and told her he just could not believe that my numbers had raised so much in one day - perhaps they had misread the lab report.

Needless to say, that didn't go over well. The nurse called the chief surgeon who then called Bill and insisted that I return to the hospital. Bill again refused! The doctor then told Bill that we all needed to talk and he wanted us to come by his office the next morning. Bill agreed. Bill was adamant, but his faith was strong. Was this another detour?

The next morning we went to the surgeon's office and Bill was counting on getting chewed out. He knew that doctors were not used to having someone disagree with them especially when it came to the technical part of lab work. As we entered the doctor's office - a calm before the storm - we had already braced ourselves for the doctor's lecture. To our surprise, the doctor informed us that he had received and reviewed the lab numbers and that Bill had been correct! The nurse had turned the numbers around. My numbers had not increased to a dangerous level, but had decreased drastically! *(The unspoken question, "Am I well enough to go home?")* Then the doctor shocked us with unexpected news. He asked, **"How would you like to go home today?"** We all just looked at each other with amazement! God had performed a huge miracle right in front of our eyes. Bill's unfaltering faith had been vindicated. We all grinned and praised the Lord for His greatness and His faithfulness!

Spiritually, our lives are like that. We start out on the journey with God after we are saved and it becomes familiar to us. We get in our comfort zone. We go to the same church, attend the same Sunday school class, listen to our pastor preach and teach, and we serve in our area of ministry. Life is good and life is without many surprises spiritually. Then something happens and spiritually we are not ready for change in our comfort zone. The upheaval this change makes brings new anxieties, new challenges and new things with which to deal. By and large, most people do not like change, so this detour can be an unwelcome event in our spiritual journey.

But think for a moment, what if God never redirected your path? What if God never walked with you on a spiritual detour? Where would your spiritual growth and Christian walk end up? Look at Paul's words:

> *12. Wherefore let him who thinks he stands today take heed that he does not fall tomorrow. 13. No test has come your way but such as is common to man: God is faithful, who will not permit you to be tempted beyond your endurance; but will with each test also show you a way of escape, so that you may be victorious.*
> *(2 Corinthians 10:12, 13 EDNT)*

Paul's words are all about spiritual detours and why God allows them in our lives. When believers think they have arrived in their spiritual walk, they become prime targets for Satan to trip up and cause them to stumble. That is why God

warns us in these verses to *take heed that he does not fall.*
God does not want us to stumble or fall and He knows that
Satan is always laying a trap for us along the path. God uses
detours in our spiritual lives to keep us from falling and to keep
us from relying on ourselves instead of trusting Him!

Notice also that He states that *No test has come
your way but such as is common to man* or no temptation
that has overcome you that is not common to other
people. Sometimes we think that our temptations are out
of the ordinary, but they are not. Through all of this, God is
faithfully watching over us guiding our steps along the path
of righteousness.   Laying out the path He wants us to walk to
reach the destination He has planned for us. This verse also
states that *with each test also show you a way of escape, so
that you may be victorious.* He will with the temptation also
make a way to escape. What does that mean? It means that
God already has a detour planned to keep you from falling or
being put into a position of no other choice but giving into the
temptation. God makes a way of escaping the temptation by
taking another route or a new course of action.

Think about that for a moment, God plots our journey
in this life and He even plans our detours to keep us from
getting side tracked by various temptations we encounter. Now
that is a God that is truly looking out for His children! The next
time you face a sudden detour in your journey, stop and begin
to look to God in full assurance knowing that He is in control
of all things, even our detours! This kind of understanding
goes a long way toward making us the dependent believers
that God wants us to be. We are to be dependent on His

leadership and not our own strength. We are to be dependent on what He knows rather than our limited knowledge of the circumstances.

Once again, it is all about relationship! As we build and develop our relationship with God, trust becomes a way of life in our spiritual walk. Trusting God matures us and develops us into the believers that He wants us to become!

Detours are not something to be dreaded nor are they routes that we need to resist in our walk with God. They should be opportunities for God to prove Himself to us once again! During these detours God can and will show us great and mighty things, if we will just look to Him with sincere faith and unwavering trust! Think for a moment, if you did not have God's detours in your spiritual journey, how much of life that God wants you to see and experience would you miss? Do not be afraid of detours!

WALKING WITH MISS KAY

14

THE UNKNOWN

The difficulty in life is the choice.
—George Moore

There are times when people who are unknown to us can have major impact on our lives. For me that happened twice! Both of my pancreas donors were from cadavers or people who had died due to illness or accidents and their families had donated their organs for others to use for transplants. The first pancreas was lost so quickly and was difficult for us to know what to say to that family. Certainly, they had gone through a great deal of heartache in deciding to offer their loved one's organs for donation. Consequently, when the organ rejected, we did not contact the family because their gift of life had not been a success.

The second pancreas transplant was different. We sent a letter to the donor family through the Kidney Foundation to the grieving family. In the letter we expressed deep sorrow for their loss and gratitude for their unselfish decision to assist others so they might have a better life. Writing that letter was difficult because somewhere in this country a family was experiencing the greatest heartache parents can ever know.

All we knew was their daughter was just 24 years old and had lost her life through an unexpected accident: a parent's worst nightmare!

So if you are in the midst of a terrible situation or circumstance, remember, it is during these times that God reaches into our lives, not only through those we love, but also by using those who are unknown to us to bring strength and comfort in the midst of trouble.

This is exactly what God did for me and my family. My husband and a dear friend, Carol, both gave me a kidney. Perhaps even more amazing, two people unknown to me through their sacrifice impacted my life through a donated pancreas. Their families were called on to make a most difficult decision. Yet, God's grace was working in their lives just as He was in mine! God is watching over you and He is listening to your cry for relief.

The eyes of the Lord are upon the righteous, and His ears are open unto their cry. (Psalms 34:15) As we cry out to God in prayer, He listens and His love goes into action! God wants to comfort you in whatever trial you are going through, but He will not act unless you permit His grace to work in your life. Open your heart to His love and grace, and then you will experience just how wonderful and comforting God's love can be! God's love is eternal!

Love is an action verb and God always puts His love into action when His children are in need. His ultimate promise is eternal life with the Saints in heaven. Here are the words of a song written by a pioneer preacher early in his ministry. These 100 year old words remain true today and bring hope and peace to all believers:

Look, Pilgrims are landing where angels are standing
On harbors of transparent gold,
The beauties of glory surpass every story
That mortal has dreamed of or told:
What joy and what rapture as heaven we capture
By sailing through stormiest gale.
They feared not the riding for God's hand was guiding,
And His breath was fanning the sails.
Such consolation with rough sails shaking
While angry winds and waves roar.
Just to know the Master is carefully steering;
The ship safely toward Heaven's shore

— R. P. Johnson

Some may be disillusioned and bitter and may think God does not care about your heartache or that He is not there in your times of hardship and suffering. You are mistaken! God is there and is actively reaching out to you to comfort in ways that only His grace can. He knows all about you. God's comfort is His grace in action!

3. Praise God, even the Father of our Lord Jesus Christ, the Father of compassion, and the God who stands beside you to encourage; 4. Who stands beside us to encourage during any kind of affliction that we in turn may be able to encourage others every time afflictions arise, by the consolation we received of God. 5. As the sufferings of Christ overflows to us, our consolation and encouragement flows from Christ. 6. And if we have miserable problems, it is for your reassurance and deliverance, that if you suffer the same difficulties you can be encouraged that we were made free from worry

to the effect that you can be delivered. 7. Our hope is
firmly grounded in you, knowing, that as you share in
our sufferings you will also share in our encouragement.
(2 Corinthians 1:3-4 EDNT)

These verses outline how God goes about the business of comforting His children. Notice verse three states that He is the God of compassions and encouragement. Have you ever realized that the comfort that you experience comes from the hand of God?

First, look at the word *comfort*. It means *to give strength and hope to; to ease the grief or trouble of; and a feeling of relief or encouragement.* Now let's put those thoughts into the text of these verses. God is the God of all comfort: He is the God who gives us strength in times of trouble and lessens our grief. He is the God who eases our troubles and gives us a feeling of relief and the encouragement we need the most! God cares about His children and is active in the life of believers. We are not forsaken in times of grief or trouble; it is then that God is most active in our lives! Jehovah will never forget you. Look at His Word in Isaiah:

15. Can a woman forget her suckling child, that
she should not have compassion on the son of her
womb? Yea, they may forget,yet will I not forget
*thee. 16. Behold, I have **graven thee upon the***
palms of my hands; thy walls are continually
***before me.** (Isaiah 49:15-16 KJV)*

15

HOME

God destines us for an end beyond the grasp of reason.
—Thomas Aquinas

There is something wonderful about coming home after you've been away for a long time! Home is a special place for all of us and it certainly is to me. I feel so secure there and at peace there. It's a different place than any other place on earth for me!

After my second transplant, finally we were allowed to go home! What a wonderful day that was. We boarded our plane for the journey home and I was so excited about getting home to see my family and my little buddy Buster! Just the thought of going home brought a big smile to my face and I think I smiled all the way home.

When we were landing at our local airport (located about two miles from our house) we saw this huge group of people standing upon the observation deck. We talked about how there sure were a lot of people waiting on loved ones on this plane!

Much to our surprise, and keep in mind this is a Wednesday night around 11 PM, that huge group was our family and friends from church! What a great surprise! Home and being greeted by so many of the people that I love the most! That made my trip home even more special.

That trip home reminds me of how it will be one day for believers! We will be called by our Savior and we'll leave this place of such sorrow. We will lift from this earth and rise to meet Him in the air. Those that have already died in Christ will receive their new glorified bodies and we'll meet them in the air.

We too will take on new bodies, bodies without the stains of this world. Bodies free from sin and we'll be free from the things that have so hindered us. Bodies without disease, without the limitations of aging and without the damage that has been caused by a lifetime of living!

Life with a healthy pancreas changes a person's life so much and in so many ways. No more insulin shots and no more days of feeling as bad as my sugar levels would swing from low to high. It was truly amazing the new world that opened up to me.

As with any transplant, there are issues to be addressed and difficulties with which to deal. Anti-rejection meds must be monitored and there are so many other drugs that have to be taken just to counteract what's going on in your body as it adjusts to the new organ.

Once we returned home, almost daily I was either going to my kidney specialist or one of my other team of doctors. Sometimes I grew so weary of all the running and all the blood work and the constant tests that had to be performed in order to manage my new found health. Many have asked me, "Was it worth it?" Without hesitation, I reply, "Yes!" After several months, the doctors appointments begin to occur less often and so does all the blood work. I began to level out concerning my health and actually began to enjoy my new life!

That reminds me of what happens when a lost person is saved. New life begins and it's just an amazing difference! That single event in our life, receiving Christ, begins to change everything! We go from a life of fear to a life of faith! We go from being dead spiritually to being alive in Christ! We are changed not only in our spirits but our souls are affected as well. We begin to look at things differently and begin to view our world differently. We no longer just focus on ourselves, but we see those with needs around us. We begin to focus our lives on Christ and His will and purpose for our living rather than just doing what we want to do. Life doesn't revolve around life's ups and downs just as my life had with my diabetic problems. Spiritually we begin to stabilize and become grounded in the Word of God. The Holy Spirit begins the process of growth and matures us into the image of Christ!

Facing life's problems and its challenges with Christ in your heart means that we are no longer facing those problems and challenges on our own. Now we have the God of all that exists with us and for us! He is a constant comfort and He ever makes intercession for us!

In Christ, all things have become new! The old things of our past life in the flesh are gone and the new life that God has planned for us is before us! Isn't that exciting? To know that God has a plan for your life and it's not subject to problems, difficulties or the ups and downs of our life! Our reason for living now revolves around our Savior! To Christ be all the glory and honor!

16

RUNNING WITH PATIENCE

*Christian, remember the goodness of God
in the frost of adversity.*
—Charles Spurgeon

In Hebrews, Paul uses an athletic analogy to help us understand the physical aspect of running the spiritual race. What an amazing Scripture!

1. Therefore, since we are watched from above by such a cloud of witnesses, let us rid ourselves of all that weighs us down, and the sin that so persistently surrounds us, and let us run with steadfast endurance, the course that is marked out before us, 2. let this fix your eyes on Jesus, the origin and the crown of all faith, who, to win His prize of blessedness, endured the cross and made light of its shame, Jesus, who now sits on the right of God's throne. 3. Consider Him who steadfastly endured such opposition at the hands of sinners, and compare your lives with His, so that you may not faint and grow weary in your souls. (Hebrews 12:1-3 EDNT)

Paul describes a person running in a race and what has to be done to be competitive and reach the goal of winning. First, Paul explains that in the race called life there are many witnesses (heroes of the faith) who are cheering us on! Just as when the streets of a city have crowds of people lined up to catch a glimpse of the runners, believers also have crowds of witnesses (those who have witnessed and experienced the grace of God in their own race) to cheer us on to victory!

Oswald Chambers once said, *Faith never knows where it is being led, but it loves and knows the One who's leading.* I love that statement and it has stuck with me through the years. Faith does not always know what is around the next corner, but it is about knowing and believing that God is with us when we turn that corner!

*Let us rid ourselves of all that weighs us down, and the sin that so persistently surrounds us, and let us run with steadfast endurance...*these are not easy words to live by. For believers to identify and lay aside all those things that ensnare or hinder our spiritual race is not such an easy matter. Jesus never implied that it would be easy any more than His going to the Cross was easy. Our spiritual lives are full of struggles day-by-day. It is a battle that will not end until Jesus takes us home!

For the next several years my life changed drastically. My health greatly improved and my life without diabetes and without all its complications was wonderful! My new pancreas and Bill's kidney performed well. My doctors monitored my med levels and constantly watched for any signs of rejection or for any complications. For the first time in my adult life I felt free to just enjoy life! I could eat anything I wanted to without the fear of how it would impact my blood sugar levels. The gift that God had given me through my transplants was beyond my power to express. I could drive again, travel and do about anything I wanted without fear of how it would impact my health. Life truly became a joy!

Then the unthinkable happened! It started in 2005, some 5 years after my successful pancreas transplant. My body began to have problems with my main anti-rejection medication, which caused another series of problems. In the end, I lost Bill's kidney 6 years after the transplant.

On July 5, 2005 I had an implant inserted so that I could begin dialysis. The next day, the first dialysis began a nine month ordeal that I would not wish on anyone! Every week, Monday, Wednesday and Friday I would go to the local dialysis unit to receive treatment. What a dreadful time that was. I went from doing well and enjoying life to now being constrained to dialysis three times a week. I could not really plan any trips because that would mean I would have to set up a time for dialysis treatment wherever I went. Dialysis limited my life in ways I never thought possible. By the day of dialysis, I was feeling the sluggishness that goes with not having a functional kidney. You feel weary and tired from the toxins in your system. Dialysis totally wears you out. The next day you feel pretty good only to realize that come morning the toxins would be back and all the symptoms that go with needing dialysis.

Such was my life for nine months! My mom had retired early so that she could help out and that was a great blessing for the family. I do not know what we would have done without mom. She was my strength during a time of weakness. She was there every time the family needed her and I knew that she was committed to helping us through this terrible time.

Good days of health and energy were now just a fleeting memory. What God had given me for those 5 years was a blessing that was certainly missed. I think we all take for granted those really good gifts that God gives us. It seems that it is human nature to dwell on the "issues" of life rather than being thankful for all the good that God gives us. I certainly missed my five years of wellness.

With the kidney failure and dialysis, once again we started the process of searching for a kidney donor. I knew that if I had to go on the national donor list, most likely it would take three years or longer for a match to be found. That is a long time on dialysis and one that I really could not endure. So, when our church family found out what was going on with my kidney, people began to tell me they would be willing to be tested and be a donor if they were a match! That just blew me away! To think of all these people that were willing to be tested and possibly go through surgery to give me a kidney was more than my mind could comprehend.

By the time I went to see my doctor I had a list of close to 30 names on it! They told me when someone comes in with possible donors it's one or two names and those are usually family members. When I handed the list of names, they said that I must really be loved. Thank God for good church friends.

God has blessed me with a loving family and a church family that loves me, too.

They began to test the possible donors on my list, but right away there was a problem. With each of my possible donors one certain antigen kept showing up and that caused concern. That anti-body could cause rejection of the donated kidney, which was a risk that no one was willing to take. It is difficult enough to ask someone to donate an organ for transplanting, but to do so with the knowledge it could be lost to rejection is just too much to ask!

As we got to the end of the testing, my doctor came to me and informed me of the best possible matches. Each of them had this anti-body, but these were the best of the possible matches. There was one procedure that could take this anti-body out of the way: IVIG treatment would reduce the number of anti-bodies out of their system, which in turn would enable my body to accept the organ without rejection. It was still a risky possibility, but it gave us the best chance that we had. After praying about the issue and talking to my doctors, I decided that Carol, a lady from my Sunday school class and a dear friend would be the one that I would ask to take the IVIG treatments and possibly be a donor. Little did I know that Carol had committed to helping me years before this crisis time in my life! Carol really had a desire and she was proactive. She went to her doctor and had a complete physical and asked him, can I offer to do this for her? After completing the physical, he told her she could add her name to the list to be considered as a donor! *Carol, became Miss Kay's second kidney donor.*

That part of the story is related in Carol's own words. It simply validates that God is working in every area of our lives, even those things that have not yet happened.

When we went to our first Women of Faith conference, Kay started to get sick. I didn't know her that well then but she became so sick and I felt so sorry for her. I began to pray and asked the Lord if there was something I could do to help her........then help me to do it!

As the years have passed, Kay and I have gotten much closer. When the time came and she had to have another kidney transplant, I just knew it was supposed to be me! I was the first one tested and the first one turned down! When they first said I couldn't be Kay's donor, I was confused. I was so sure that God had told me I was the one. All I knew to do was to pray, so I did! I began to pray, God, whatever is best for her, your will be done. But if you can allow me to do this, I am willing.

*Others were tested, but the same antigen was blocking some of us from being a better match up. So what it came down to was they were going to try to do an IVIG treatment that would help to remove the antibodies that had been identified as being antibodies that would lead to rejection. **So they asked Kay concerning those who had been tested, which one she would rather try to become her donor. Her response was Carol!***

I had no second thoughts about being Kay's donor. I was a little nervous and excited for her at the same time! I didn't want her to go through this anymore. She's been through so much and she had hit one brick wall after another one! I didn't want any more dialysis for Kay, nor did I want Bill or Georgia to go through any more. They are the best people in the world and if I could just take away some of that, it would be worth it.

My family was fine with my decision to be a donor. My husband was behind me all the way! I felt like God had given me this as a blessing. You always want to help the people you love, to go the extra mile, to give of yourself. Not many people get to give the gift that I was able to give. It was truly a blessing to me! —**Carol**

Hannah is Carol's daughter. She was just 14 when her mother gave me a kidney. This young teen expresses in her own words her emotions about the transplant.

The day of Mom's surgery was full of emotions. I was worried for both Mom and Kay, but also excited that it would hopefully be the last time that Kay would go through something like this. I thank God that He let my Mom have the opportunity to have such an impact on someone else's life. —**Hannah**

My doctor at Vanderbilt wanted me to have a heart test done to be certain that my heart was strong enough for another transplant. I had no symptoms of heart problems but a heart cauterization revealed I had three blockages! Due to being a diabetic for 32 years, the wear and tear on my blood vessels had caused this blockage. Two of the vessels had a 50% blockage and the third had a 95% blockage!

The decision was made that I would need surgery to put in a stint in the blood vessel with 95% blockage. My options were: no stint put in, no transplant or put the stint in and hope for the best! My doctors told me that most likely without the stint that I'd have a heart attack during the transplant.

But the other issue was that by putting in the stint it would delay my transplant by at least three months, which

I did not want to do! It was one of those times where you know what you need to do but it is not what you want to do. Have you ever been in a similar circumstance? It is not easy to be a patient and just do what you know you "should do." I wanted the transplant so I would no longer need dialysis and so my health could improve. In my mind, I thought, here we go again, another brick wall. Carol also had to have certain tests done to make sure everything was OK with her physically for the transplant to go forward. She passed every test except she spilled a little protein in her urine. The staff stated it is not enough to be concerned for her health, but it is enough to stop her from being a possible donor! I thought, here we go again!

They wanted to run the test again due to Carol being so determined to be my donor! Bill started doing research on the Internet about possible causes of protein being spilled in the urine. One of the things he found was that eating a lot of chicken can cause protein to show up in your urine. Carol loved chicken and a lady at our church who is a nurse told her to get lots of rest before the test. Carol almost went on a bread-and-water diet before the second test and even sat on the couch for 3 days just so the test would come back OK! Now that is determination!

The second test came back so good that even the staff were a little confused. So, they had it repeated a third time. Again, the test came back perfect; no protein being spilled in her urine. Carol was thrilled that she had been chosen for the treatment and to possibly be my donor. Now the treatments would begin and we would have to see if the treatments worked in reducing the anti-bodies. It wasn't long before the tests revealed that the IVIG treatments had reduced the anti-bodies! Now we were ready to schedule surgery and move toward my fourth transplant! Isn't God great? Problem after problem and yet God took care of every issue. That is the kind of God we serve. One who is there right now working for us every minute of every day!

There were still problems that I faced. Six weeks before my transplant my doctor had taken out the old kidney in hopes of putting my new one in its place. We were then informed that I had hardening of the arteries (calcification) and the artery that had been used to supply blood to my former kidney was no longer acceptable. The artery had become diseased and would most likely not hold up to another kidney being stitched to it. The doctor went on to explain that we faced the same possibility with other arteries. They too could be diseased and might not be healthy enough for a graph.

As we left the doctor's office that day, I was so upset. We had hit one obstacle after another and it just seemed to never end. The calcification with a long-term diabetic is different from the average person. Diabetes attacks the lining of the blood vessel and the walls of the vessel begin to thicken causing the blood flow to be restricted. They cannot go into the vessel and clean them out as they normally would because that is not the real problem.

We went back to our hotel in Nashville that afternoon and God began to deal with my heart. I was reminded of one Scripture after another which dealt with this new problem.

(John 11:40) When Lazarus had died and Mary and Martha were so upset that Jesus had not arrived in time. Martha said, Lord, he has been dead four days and he stinketh by now. Here Jesus was ready to raise Lazarus from the dead. Jesus saith to her, *said I not unto thee, that if thou wouldst believe, thou should see the glory of God.*

I thought, "Lord, this is going to be a hard transplant. And there are a lot of complications and risks involved, but I need to believe. And I believe we will see the glory of God."

Naturally I thought of Peter, stepping out of that boat then looking at his circumstances. God, help me to have sufficient faith. Then some of my favorite verses came to mind:

I will lift up my eyes unto the hills from whence cometh my help. My help cometh from the Lord, which made heaven and earth. **(Psalms 121:1-2)**

I wait for the Lord, my soul doth wait, and in his word do I hope. **(Psalms 130:5)**

Fear thou not, for I am with thee. Be not dismayed for I am thy God. I will strengthen thee, I will help thee, yea, I will uplift thee with the right hand of my righteousness. **(Isaiah 41:10)**

They that wait upon the Lord shall renew their strength. They shall mount up with wings of eagles. They shall run and not be weary, and they shall walk and not faint. **(Isaiah 40:31)**

God used all those verses and others to help and strengthen me. I lay there that night thinking about different things that God had been speaking to my heart. I kept thinking, God is in control and all through this transplant we have hit so many **brick walls**.

Then there was **(Isaiah 49:15, 16)**:

*Can a woman forget her suckling child, that she should not have compassion on the son of her womb? Yea, they may forget, **yet will I not forget thee**. Behold, I have graven thee upon the palms of my hands; **thy walls are continually before me.***

I realized that God would never forget me, that I was engraved in the palms of His Hands, and He knew all about "my walls" be they brick and mortar or disappointment, heartaches, or disease. God desires to show His power and might. Because when this thing does happen—and I believed it was going to happen—we will see great and mighty things from God! I believe God is showing us great and mighty things right now!

We all went to bed and it was one of those nights we could not sleep. At 4:30 AM we decided to pack up and go home. We left Nashville about 5:30 AM and headed home to Kingsport. When we arrived, Bill was there. He was very supportive, as he always is. He said, you want to go to the Christian bookstore? So we went shopping for Adena's birthday coming up the next week. It kind of helped to get my mind off things.

We went to church that night and everyone was supportive and strong in their faith that God was going to make this happen! And my mom's faith that day and night, even though she was devastated too, was strong and she kept encouraging me. So did Jimmy and Ethel, the couple that had driven me to Nashville.

My little grandson, Dylan, was just five years old at the time of this trial. His Sunday school teacher came up to me and said, "You would not believe Dylan's prayers! They are so sincere and he doesn't ramble, he prays from the heart!" When you ask Dylan to pray about something, he bows his little head and prays about the issue right then! He doesn't waste time. He prayed every single night for his mamaw to get a new kidney and to feel better. I get a lot of support from Dylan. He asked me once, "Mamaw, when you get your new kidney, will you feel like playing with me more?" I said, "Yes, honey, we'll play all you want!" I enjoy our special time together. I have such a beautiful support system through my family, our friends and our church family.

The next morning I called my transplant coordinator with a few questions. She said, "I really feel good about this. Dr. Schaffer is meticulous and in most of these cases he dismisses them and will not even attempt the transplant. He has to feel pretty good about it or he would not put you through all this."

Soon I received a call and was informed that the transplant team had met with a vascular surgeon to see if he would be on call the day of surgery in case we ran into some problems related to my blood vessels. The vascular doctor agreed to be on hand if needed and Dr. Schaffer was on board with attempting the transplant! The surgery was set for March 16, 2006. We were going to leave from home on Wednesday, March 15th to travel to Vanderbilt in Nashville, TN, which is about a 4-½ hour drive. The day we left for surgery was my husband's birthday, March 15th. He and another lady from church, Joan Lindamood, had birthday's in March. She said, "I've never asked you for anything for my birthday, but this time, I'm asking for something. I want you to have a successful transplant." My husband said the same thing, "that's all I want for my birthday."

My regular dialysis days were Tuesday, Thursday & Saturday. I dialyzed on Tuesday, March 14th, and then I also dialyzed on Wednesday, the 15th, the day before surgery. They want you to dialyze as close as possible before surgery, because they want you after dialysis has pulled off the poisons and excess fluids.

In all our minds, there was no *if* about the new transplant; it would be successful. Carol and I felt strongly and so did Mom and my husband, everybody had good feelings about the process. After we said our goodbyes, we were on our way to Vanderbilt in Nashville. When we arrived, we checked into the Holiday Inn and then we all went to eat together and we talked and laughed and had good fellowship with Don, Carol, Hannah, Bill, my mother and me.

After we ate, we went back to the hotel, and their room was straight across the hall from us, so we were right there together. In preparation for the surgery, Carol had to drink 96 ounces of fluid before midnight. She couldn't have soda pop or fruit juices or anything like that but they told her she could have tea. Well, Carol loves tea, so she decided to drink tea instead of water. We went downstairs and there was no tea to be found. There was a restaurant but let's put it this way, it's not where we were going to find tea, but we finally got Carol all the tea that she needed to drink so that we could get her prepared for surgery the next morning. They didn't have tea made up at the Holiday Inn so they had to brew some and he thought it was really weird that we knew exactly how many ounces that we wanted of tea. I think we about flipped him out but later we explained. Mom, Carol and I got the tea and went back upstairs. Carol wasn't thinking that because she didn't want to drink water, she would be drinking regular tea - not decaf tea. So, naturally she was up all night; bless her heart, she had a hard time.

When we got back upstairs, we were getting ready to go to our rooms and Carol put her arm around me. You've got to understand, Carol is really tall and I'm really short. She threw her arm around me and said, "I just don't see how they're going to get my big kidney, as tall as I am, into your little body", and I said, "Oh, believe me, it will work. They'll get it in there." She's crazy!

The next morning we had to be at Vanderbilt at 5:30. We all met in our room at 5:00 and we stood in a circle, Don, Carol, Hannah, Bill, Momma and I, and we held hands and we prayed together. Don led us in prayer. We all left for the hospital feeling really, really good about the surgery. We went to admitting and of course Vanderbilt is very emotional for me because that's where my Daddy was for all of his surgeries before he died with throat cancer. It just brings back so many memories and to actually walk into that building and the waiting room; everything's so familiar. It's so emotional for me.

We got there on time and went into admitting with Mom and Hannah staying in the surgery waiting area. We hugged them and told them we loved them! Carol, Don, Bill and I went to Pre-Op. When we got to Pre-Op, they sent Bill and Don over into a waiting room until they got Carol and I ready.

Afterwards they allowed Bill and Don to come back in with us. Carol and I walked into Pre-Op arm in arm and we stayed arm in arm standing there until they were ready to get started preparing us for surgery. They put us side by side in pre-op. We were right next to each other with just a curtain drawn between us until they were done inserting our IV's and seeing the anesthesiologist. Once we had all that complete, we could pull the curtain and talk.

I know one time I pulled the curtain back so I could see her – to see what she was doing. Anyway, we were laying side by side and at one point I pulled the curtain back and said, "How are you doing?", and she said, "fine". I said, "Are you sure that you want to do this, are you sure you want to go through with this?" I had asked her this several times in the past few weeks and I got the same answer every time. She said, "Yes, I'm sure. Stop asking me. I am sure. I feel very strong about doing this. I know that I'm the one called to do it and I have a real deep desire to do it." She would say, "We're going to get this done and you will be better and you will be off dialysis and we're going to be ready to go to Women of Faith in June." So all the way, her response was strong and said, "I want to do this." Soon Bill and Don were allowed back into pre-op and the curtains were still pulled. Don and Carol were talking with Bill and I on the other side. It was getting close to time that they would put us both to sleep.

The surgeons would start on me first. Usually, it's just the opposite – they put the donor to sleep and start operating on the donor first and then part way through hers, they open me up to get me ready to receive the kidney. Since we weren't sure that I could even be transplanted with a new kidney because of the calcification around my blood vessels, they didn't want to have to cut on Carol if not necessary. If they got in there and saw that they could do the surgery and found a good place for it to sit and to have good blood flow to it, then, they would start on Carol. So, I would be the one first, but they would put us both to sleep and they said we would not know anything about whether the surgery went through or not until we woke up. That is when Carol said she hoped and prayed that she would wake up in pain because she would know that they would have done it.

Now it was getting close to time to be going down and be put to sleep, and you could just feel the excitement, but yet nervousness at the same time! We were all believing God all the way. I had peace. I had total peace about it, but there was just an excitement in the air that was just hard to describe. I had peace, perfect peace, but yet I was so ready for it to be over. Maybe it was just the dread of the surgery, but it was finally happening! We had waited so very, very, very long and had run into so many obstacles along the way, but God is in control all the way through. His timing is perfect.

Of course I was crying and I could not stop crying or stop the tears; Bill would just wipe them away. Finally I grew quiet and Bill asked me what I was thinking. I told him that I was drawing my swords. I'm drawing my swords of the Spirit.

Our Bible is our arsenal; I learned that from David Jeremiah. Our Bible is our arsenal and it is full of swords! They were just swords of assurance, swords of God's love and peace and how mighty He is.

Bill said let's just draw some swords together, so we started drawing swords together and we came up with some really great scripture together. The Lord gave us some wonderful swords to draw. I told Bill I'm not crying because I'm scared." I said I have perfect peace about the transplant and I'm not afraid, but my tears are just my emotions for my feelings for Carol and for the great sacrifice that she was making for me. I just couldn't stop the tears with her laying there beside of me and after all the preparation; all the time that we had put into this and all the prayer put into it; it was finally here. It was finally time and when she was laying there beside of me, the reality of what she was getting ready to do for me just hit so hard I couldn't stop the tears ... I just couldn't stop the tears.

Carol is such a loving person and she is so loving and protective of me. She could not stand to see me on dialysis; to see me sick and feeling bad all the time. She had such a desire to see me off dialysis and feeling better. She has such a giving spirit. She helps everybody. Our friendship and our love for each other are very strong, and it was very strong before all of this. She's just a very special lady.

Now it was 7:30 and time to go to surgery. They came and got Carol first and as they rolled her out of Pre-Op, we were throwing I love you signs to each other in sign language. That was the most we could get out at that time. Then they came after me. Then Bill kissed me and told me he loved me and that it would be fine and that I would soon have a new kidney. Mom and Hannah were already downstairs in the surgical waiting room where Bill and Don would join them.

When my Dad had surgery, the hospital did not have a monitor listing how the surgeries were going. It was new and it was a great blessing to my family.   It showed what time it was, how long a patient had been in surgery, and how they're doing.

They began operating on me first to determine if I was able to accept an organ. My name was already on the monitor and then Mom said all of a sudden it said 'Carol Pickel'! The monitor said her name, and Mom said when I saw her name, I knew they were putting a new kidney in Kay and that they'd found a place to put it! They were all so excited, and seeing the monitor, they were able to know that the surgery was going forward and they'd found a place to put the new kidney.

After surgery, Carol woke up in pain just like she'd prayed about ...just like she had wanted to. She said the pain could've been a little less, but that's okay. Carol did wake up in pain and she thought, oh, it's happened! I woke up and my first question was do I have a new kidney. The nurse in the recovery room told me, yes! She said that Bill and Mom wanted to come in to see me. Carol had already been assigned a room, but they couldn't find me a room on the floor where I should be, which would have been the same as Carol's.

Bill said I was so out of it, that they didn't stay but a minute. They went on out to the waiting room, but I remember when they came into my room. I could feel Bill's thumb down my forehead like he does to let me know he's there. I remember waking up – do I have a new kidney I asked again. I was just so sleepy, and they told me yes. I remember that nurse and I just kept thanking her for taking such good care of me as I left the recovery room. They finally found me a room and so I went upstairs on the same floor as Carol.

The pain was severe for both Carol and me. Carol also had a lot of nausea, but it was coming from her pain. She wasn't taking her pain medicine with her little pump because she was afraid it would make her sick, which normally it would. Well, when she told the doctor that she was nauseated, and she said she wasn't using the pump, he grabbed the pump and put pain medicine in, which in turn scared her to death. He said you are nauseated because of all the pain, and sure enough, as the pain went down from the medicine, the nausea left too. She said she wished someone had told her that a long time ago! I was in pain too but they were very careful. The nurse was in the room almost all night measuring things, how much output, everything was just very strict. They were watching everything. Bill stayed with me and Don with Carol. Hannah and Mom went back to the hotel. The next day, Bill rested and Mom stayed with me and Don went to work.

The creatinine level measures the amount of toxins that your kidney is filtering out of your body and how well you're purifying your system. It measures exactly where the kidney function is, how good it is, or how bad it is. Normal is 0.5 to 1.5 and that's excellent. When I went into surgery that morning, I had a 7 creatinine level, and by 5:30 that afternoon after surgery, it was down to 2. By 5:30 a.m. the next morning,

Friday, it was down to 1.1 and Saturday at 5:30 a.m., it was down to 0.7. We were thrilled and couldn't believe it!

Carol went home on Saturday and I went home on Sunday. I remember the first time that Carol and I saw each other after surgery. She'd gotten up Friday out of her bed and very slowly made it to my room to see me. I really can't explain seeing her for the first time after the surgery and how I felt. It was like there was a bond created there that, even though we were already bonded so strongly, there was a special bond and I remember having that with my husband after he donated his kidney during my first transplant. As our eyes met and we knew how successful everything was so far, it was just an excitement and a thrill way deep down in your soul that you know only God can give.

God gave that special bond between me and Carol, and we knew that He had just performed a total miracle! To be able to explain the feeling after knowing I had her kidney and it was functioning perfectly, it's just indescribable! I really couldn't put it into words. It was just awesome.

I came home late Sunday afternoon and had to be back at Vanderbilt early Wednesday morning to do one more IVIG treatment. When the nephrologist did my labs for that day, she came down to see me and none of us could believe it, but my creatinine level was 0.4, which is better than a person with two healthy kidneys! I was told Vanderbilt had four other people that they did IVIG treatments on like me and three of them had rejected. Of course they were afraid I would do the same thing because I was so high risk. When our God does something, He does it right! I **did not** reject and I'm over two years out as I write today! By the time this book comes out, a lot more time will pass. I have suffered no rejection whatsoever and have maintained at this point a 0.8 to 0.9 creatinine level, which is absolutely perfect.

Dr. Schaffer was so meticulous and such a wonderful doctor. And then Dr. Heidi Schaffer, the doctor who now treats me after the transplant, I just can't say enough about her. She was expecting during this time, but she is so down to earth and so funny. We laughed. We talked about our dogs. She's got a black lab named Harley, and at the time, we had one Maltese named Gracie who is a 1 ½ years old and now we have Cody who is 3 months old. I showed her pictures of Gracie in her Easter dress and she got the biggest kick out of that. She's a great doctor and I just think she's wonderful. I am glad God sent her my way.

I have been blessed with wonderful doctors. My family doctor, Dr. Daniel Carol, there's no way there could be a better doctor. He's a wonderful Christian man, he's a concerned man, and he's an extremely intelligent man. He's concerned about his patients and very understanding. I just thank God for the doctors He has put in my life.

Dr. Steven Butler, my nephrologist in Kingsport, Tennessee, my hometown, is so intelligent and he's just so good. He's wonderful at what he does and just such a good doctor.

I started feeling so much better and things were really starting to turn around now because I felt like I could start to heal. God had really performed two miracles. One, no rejection when all I had heard was how high risk I was for rejection, and two, they were able to put that kidney exactly where they had taken my husband's out! God had taken care of every issue concerning this transplant! This is a poem that Bill wrote for me while I was on dialysis.

Heroes Often Walk Among Us

There comes within our life
Those who endure so much strife;
We witness their fears, struggles and pain,
But their faith walks in the sun and not in the rain.

Our Father from above looks down through the eyes of His love.
He plants us heroes in the paths of our life,
That we might know how He sustains us in the midst of strife.
How can it be with these with faith so great
Walk so unstained in this world of hate.
Their faith has been tempered through the fire
Their circumstances they've experienced so dire.

Heroes often walk among us,
The value they bring is such a plus.
Heroes often walk among us
As they are used to touch our life
I know, for the hero God sent my way
is my wife.

—Bill Christian

17

DEATH CASTS A LONG SHADOW

*You can't see anything properly
while your eyes are blurred with tears.*

—C. S. Lewis

The phone rang at 4:30 A.M. and instantly my senses
were on alert. The call was the type a parent never wants to
get. At first, I did not understand or realize what the doctor
had just told me. I could not comprehend how bad it was. So
the doctor once again explained all the details. There was still
hope, a remote chance, but the prognosis for Adena was not
good. Tears fell as they had never fallen before. The doctor
was talking about my "baby," my youngest daughter. This
cannot be! This should not be! Dee was too young, only 29
years old. How could this be?

Traveling to Chattanooga, TN., the closer we got to
Erlanger hospital, the more my heart raced with anxiety and
my stomach became more upset. The last few miles of travel
were almost unbearable. After what seemed an eternity,
we arrived at the ICU. They took us to our daughter's bed
and I honestly thought my heart would stop, just cease to
function. Adena was wrapped in an ice suit, on life support

and the medical staff was trying special measures to keep the swelling from damaging her brain. Adena had fallen in the commons hall at school but no one realized just how seriously she was hurt. Shortly after the fall, she had a seizure, and an ambulance was called. While en-route to Erlanger Hospital, she had more seizures in the ambulance, and her heart stopped. CPR was performed, the heart was shocked, and her heart started beating again. When she arrived at the ER, her heart stopped again. Again her heart was shocked and CPR was administered, but this time for over 45 minutes. Ten minutes of CPR is going the extra mile to save an individual, but the staff at Erlanger had gone well beyond the normal procedure in an attempt to save our daughter's life. For this we are grateful.

As with all accidents or illness that places a loved one in ICU, waiting is difficult. At this point, Adena's eyes were still responsive to light, so there was still a possibility of her waking up! Our thoughts, as with most parents who are believers, were that our Lord will come through for us. He will touch her and she will wake up, and everything will be fine...or maybe not! Tragic situations often turn emotions inside out. As C. S. Lewis wrote, *"You can't see anything properly while your eyes are blurred with tears."* The long and terrible wait began.

Dark clouds of sorrow were hanging heavy over us and the possibility of death was already casting a long shadow over our lives. Why? Why? That little word just kept going through my mind. I want my baby back! Please God, give my baby back! Please let her wake up and be fine. Please! I prayed for those big beautiful green eyes to open and see my face. Yet, these comforting words of Helen Keller were in the back of my mind: *"Reinforced by faith, the weakest mortal is mightier than disaster. Faith directs to the light when darkness prevails."* Helen Keller was blind from birth and lived in darkness, yet by faith was directed to the light.   The question was - can we weather the biggest storm of our lives? All of the other hardships our family had endured paled in comparison to this one. The suffering of a child...the loss of a child is a difficult storm for parents to endure.

Storms often come when things are calm. Life was fairly calm at this time in our family. God had just taken our daughter through a mighty battle and our whole family was rejoicing in God's blessings. Adena seemed to be finally turning her life in a positive direction for the first time in a long time. Then this unplanned event and this unexpected accident happened and it was just like getting the wind knocked out of you. We had been through many spiritual battles trying to rescue our daughter from the dark storms that kept assaulting her life. Maybe this is the reason this sudden and unforeseen storm was so bewildering and was so painful to us.

It seems that every tornado has its own color, sound, and shape. When thinking along these lines, it occurred that the **color** kind of represented the strength of the storm and certainly this storm was dark, and the intensity was extremely personal! The **sound** reminds me that a storm does not have to be loud to be destructive. This storm did not make much sound. Mostly it would be best described as a quiet storm. The sound of the ICU machines doing their work to keep our daughter alive certainly were not loud, but were just consistent. All this was going on while our beautiful daughter lay there in a coma with her body limp. The **shape** of the storm, whether small or large, can be devastating. Every storm takes on a life of its own. There appears to be no sense to where the storm heads or why it appears to focus in on this house or another. The end result of the storm can be total devastation or it might just be minor damage.

All humans are tempest tossed during their life span and even sacred writings clearly show that during the "few days of life there will be many troubles." Families are not exempt from the disturbing conditions that upset the expected living conditions. When normal circumstances are disturbed and life is beset by unexpected situations, even the strongest believers often become discouraged. This is where believers must reach deep into the shelter of their faith and find strength for the rest of the journey.

At this point a family's loss of a child was a most destructive storm, the amount of damage done to Adena's life was still unknown. Certain storms are rated from F-1 to F-5..... the worst being an F-5. Our fears were toward an F-5, but we were hoping and praying for less damage. We all have storms that invade our lives at different seasons and from different directions. Although God heals the broken heart and binds up the believers wounds. Notwithstanding, that God is great and His power and understanding are infinite (Psalms 147:3 & 5), our faith was stretched to the limit.

A tornado has stages, they do not just happen. Storms develop over a period of time. During the **developing stage,** we walk in the calm before the storm. We can look back over our lives and see how God prepared us for this storm even though we had no idea it was even coming. Looking back over unusual things that happened within our little family, God was preparing us for this catastrophic storm. Through a variety of ways and by different means God had prepared us for what was ahead.

When a storm reaches its most powerful stage, it is known as the **maturing stage.** This is when one feels the full force of the threat and most of us are at a loss of how to respond. This was where we found ourselves on that tragic day! The words of Proverbs were a comfort *"Trust in the Lord with all thine heart and lean not unto thine own understanding. In all thy ways acknowledge Him, and He shall direct thy paths."* (Proverbs 3:5-6) The way my husband interprets these verses gives additional assurance*:*

> *In times of great trial, learn to trust the Lord completely. Do not put confidence into your own view of what is going on. In every area of your life, remember the God you serve and by experience you have known and what He has taught you; and He will direct you in how to respond to this situation.*

The present storm unleased on our family seemed so different from all the rest. When a storm involves a loved one, many will lose their focus and lean on their emotions. My daughter and I were best friends. We did so much together and she lived across the street which meant she was at our house daily. For me, this storm was becoming more than my life could bear.

As a storm begins to lose its strength, it is in the **descending stage**. When a person or family has been through all the stages of a storm and it begins to subside, the damage becomes obvious. However, God is always on damage control in the life and family of believers. God promised He would never leave us nor forsake us. My husband teaches about this and shares that *God will never give up on us, or never leave us helpless, nor will He abandon us.*

The damage from the head injury had caused extensive bleeding in Adena's brain. The devastation was too much for her body to overcome. She died just five days after we got the call concerning her accident. Of course we were full of questions and doubts, but the words of Helen Keller were a comfort:

> *Don't be discouraged if you are full of questions and doubts in your storm. Healthy questioning keeps faith alive and dynamic! Unless we start with doubt, we don't have a deep rooted faith. One who believes lightly and unthinkingly has not much belief or faith. Deep rooted faith cannot be shaken. People have gotten this faith through blood and tears – has worked his way from doubt to truth as one who reaches a clearing through a thicket of branches and thorns.*

In my heart I knew that my daughter was safe, but that did not mean that all was good with me. Feelings of intense anger over Adena's death were mostly directed toward God. Part of the problem was that I was unwilling to admit this and it scared me. Never before had I felt this way toward God. So my struggle was between admitting my anger toward God and facing up to it or just pretending there was no angry present at all. It is extremely hard to hide such feelings because we cannot control or make them go away. My life had been one of faith since I was saved at age nine. I was always a person of strong faith and believed and trusted God and had deep respect for His leadership in my life. So these feelings of anger were different, they were so foreign from anything I had ever known in my walk with God. I was dealing with the loss of my youngest daughter and at the same time facing feelings about God that were causing deep concern and fear for my wellbeing.

Through all my sickness and personal trials, I was secure in my faith, but this stormy episode was threatening to shake the core of my soul and destroy the foundation of my faith. There were no words or action of others that brought me comfort. There were no simple fixes for the problems that Dee's death had brought. I was feeling the piercing pangs of loss and the mental anguish that only a mother can experience. There are no pills, special treatments, or surgery to fix my troubled heart. God was the only possible answer.

Now I needed God more than ever before, but my loss had caused an estranged feeling toward God. Suffering the greatest loss I had ever known, what could I do? At first the best course seemed to avoid God, but that certainly was not the right action with my present physical needs. The silence of my mouth could not change the thunderous sorrows of my soul. So my decision had put me in a position for the devil to defeat me completely. In past situations, I was in God's Word and my sword was sharp! I knew Scripture to use to counteract what Satan was throwing at me. I was skillful in using God's

Word which helped to offset what the enemy was using against me. Now I just seemed so weak and impotent against the attacks on my faith. Yet, God was there!

At this stage, I was beyond miserable. I was unable to hide my feelings for long from family and friends, and those within our church. Finally one day while driving, I just spoke out loud to God what I had been feeling. God already knew my feelings so I decided to speak the truth myself directly to God. I needed to confess to God what was in my heart. I needed to pour out every last ounce of pain, distress, anxiety and disappointment trapped in my immortal soul. I just needed a heart to heart talk with my Heavenly Father!

Screaming at the top of my voice and pounding my steering wheel, I shouted over and over again, "Why, why, why..." Why did something so painful and hurtful have to happen? My pain was unbearable, and there were no answers to my; Why? Why? After a short time I began to quiet down. There was only silence in the car. Salty tears rushed down my cheeks. In a soft manner God broke through my confused mind and calmly spoke to my broken heart with a simple, yet infinitely profound understanding:

> *...Dee wanted her struggle to be over. She wanted to be free of the constant battle that had raged in her life for years. The fear, the depression, and the use of alcohol as she tried to cope with feelings and hurts that were far beyond her capability to control. There were so many terrible things that she had endured; she just wanted the struggle to be over. She had tried over and over again to defeat these issues in her life.*

Now, I understood; she needed a better place, a safe place in the Arms of God. I knew in my heart that Dee was saved, she had assured me many times of her relationship with God. The classmates and roommates in Chattanooga shared that Dee had been witnessing about her faith with each one. She told them the Bible stories her Dad used as illustrations to help them with their spiritual problems. They also shared that she used God's Word to counsel them, to encourage them in their spiritual journey. I was satisfied.

As God spoke to the ear of my heart that day, my soul rejoiced as I understood that Dee's battle was over! God had freed her from years of spiritual warfare and all the bad elements that had caused her such deep pain. Dee had finished her race on this earth. Even though her journey was completed at an early age, she crossed the finish line and won the victory that our Lord had promised.

If tomorrow starts without me, and I'm not there to see,
You know how much I loved you, as much as you loved me!
When tomorrow starts without me; please understand,
An angel called my name, and said,
"Your home is ready in heaven, come and see!"

When I walked through those pearly gates,
And God smiled from His throne,
He said, "This is what I promised you."
I felt right at home!

So when tomorrow starts without me
We won't be far apart.
For every time you think of me,
I am right there, in your heart!

—adapted from the work of David M. Romano

"Earth has no sorrow

that

Heaven cannot heal!"

—Thomas Moore

18

DEALING WITH PERSONAL LOSS

*We don't put death on our day planner,
but one day it just shows up.*
—Mark Cahill

*Every difficult, confusing season in life offers a
choice. You can either surrender your questions
and sorrow to God so He can use them, or you can
surrender to bitterness, to the enemy of your soul
who will use them against you. Don't give him the
weapons to hurt you. Trust God, be patient, and
even forgive Him if you need to. Humble yourself
and wrap yourself in your blanket of faith. In
doing so, you will turn your sorrow into a tool that
refines you and makes you beautiful. In doing so,
you will find meaning in your sorrow.*
—Jennifer Rothschild

Death is a most dreaded enemy and if we permit it,
death has the ability to consume us. Death is never easy; God
determines both life and death. God brings children into our
lives and when their earthly journey is complete, He calls them
home. Death visits all families and leaves its mark on each one

of us. However, the effects of death can be minimized and the grace and blessings of God can be utilized to move past the loss and enable us to cope with the grief. God is no stranger to death nor is He without compassion for those who experience the death of a child. It is in that compassion that we will find strength to sustain us and comfort us, to grow in areas that we never thought possible. If we allow the Holy Spirit to do His work within us there will be fruit and a productive life. Through this entire dark journey, God can and will receive glory, but only if we learn the life lessons we are taught about loss.

By the time you bury a loved one there is nothing left; you are completely drained and running on empty. Yet, I often think of how gracious God was during Adena's final struggle. He put support people in our path and made sure certain things were learned about the closing days of Dee's journey on earth. God wanted us to know her final steps were on the straight path and that she ended well. Now, all the weights that had so easily beset her were gone. All the pain and hurt of this life were finished, never to trouble her again! Now she could rest in the peaceful arms of Jesus and finally experience true joy. I praise our Lord for the great things He has done! He alone is worthy of honor and praise!

Elizabeth B. Brown in her book *Surviving the Loss of a Child* wrote:

> *Every year in America, 228,000 children under the age of 24 die from catastrophic illness, accident, suicide, or murder, and those statistics do not include miscarriages, stillbirths, or the deaths of those over the age of 24. Fifteen out of*

every hundred infants dies before his or her first birthday: 28,600 deaths per year due primarily to prematurity or low birth weight. In addition there are 980,000 miscarriages and stillborn baby deaths per year.

These staggering numbers impact lives every day, and many are being affected by the loss of loved ones. Parents, siblings, family members, churches and friends find themselves grief-stricken and inconsolable by human means: the only true comfort and solace will come from a personal relationship with God. Family and friends may support during the grieving process, but only divine intervention can bring the true light of God's love into a dark and troubled soul.

How a loved one died is not the real issue; the preoccupation with "how" it happened was troubling and strange to me. It seems that most people want to know "how" when you are dealing with the painful nature of loss. You will certainly encounter those who have this attitude and their questions will delay your dealing directly with the personal loss. Repeating time and again the "how" actually increases the suffering in the loss of a loved one. It is best to just acknowledge that your loved one is in a better place: that death is the ultimate healing. Death is freedom from the constraints of the human condition and provides victorious entry into Eternal Life promised to all believers. It is clear that something has to take each one out of this world and that is not the important matter: the destination of the departed one is the issue.

Sacred scripture clearly speaks to this issue, *Weep at the birth of a child for the troubles and trials that will come, but rejoice at their passing because the final battle has been won.* (Ecclesiastes 7:1) Leaving this tragic and suffering world for a better place is a good thing! Paul, at the end of his life, even though he was weak and sick, wanted to live for the benefit of others, but personally, Paul thought dying would be better. Death would take him into the eternal presence of God.

> *20. according to my earnest faith and expectation, that in nothing I shall feel guilty, but with all fluency and courage, as always, now Christ shall be magnified in my physical body, whether by life or by death. 21. Living means Christ to me and death means gain. 22. But if living in this body means more fruitful labor: yet what I shall choose I know not. 23. This is my dilemma, having a desire to depart, and to be with Christ; which is far better: 24. nevertheless to abide in this body is more necessary for you. 25. Having this confidence, I know that I shall remain and continue working for you and furthering your joy of faith; (Philippians 1:20-25 EDNT)*

Another aspect of loss is the personal pain and darkness that descends upon the family of the departed. The darkness that comes with death touches every part of our lives. For many, there is the fear that life will never be the same. And they are correct. Life without a loved one will never be exactly the same. However, when we remember that God is love and love is eternal then we begin to realize that loved ones remain loved even when they are "away"... gone to work, on a trip, or when their last trip took them past the portals of heaven. Our loved ones in Christ are not dead, but are safely in the eternal presence of God. Eternal life means an everlasting existence. We should always think of departed loved ones as being safe and at peace. This is the surest way to deal with grief.

From the human perspective, the death of a parent, a spouse, or a child is a great personal loss. It is similar to an amputation; a part of you is lost forever, but this is a purely human reaction. Believers do not weep as others who have no hope. We hope because of the Resurrection of Jesus. He lives; consequently, we and our loved ones in Christ will also live. The meaning of the word "resurrection" is to "stand up again." Those deceased loved ones your human heart counted lost will be "standing" at Heaven's Gate to welcome you! This should be cause for great rejoicing. Remember, loved ones remain "loved ones" even when they are away.

Some allow the darkness of loss to take them down the road of bitterness. Scripture considered bitterness this way: *Looking diligently lest any man fail (fall short) of the grace of God; lest any root of bitterness springing up trouble you, and thereby many be defiled.* (Hebrews 12:15) The Evergreen Devotional New Testament (EDNT) put this verse in a better light: *Watch that no one misses the grace of God; lest any cause for animosity grow up to trouble you, and thereby many be corrupted.* Bitterness, like a weed growing in a garden, is similar to emotional weeping. It begins to obstruct spiritual nurture - even before it appears it has already taken root. It has established itself, and already started spreading its vicious choking of faith. That is what bitterness tends to do to those who respond to loss by only feeding on raw human emotions. The bitterness (darkness) begins to crowd out the good fruit of life's garden and the darkness takes control and corrupts our grief.

Human emotions that naturally rise up during the loss of a loved one often become an effective weapon used to discourage and turn the heart away from God. For instance, the days after Dee's death became a blur. There were so many questions. Did God let us down? Was our faith weak? It was difficult to put things in the right time frame. There were many unknown details, and so many things to do. There were people to notify, funeral arrangements to work out and all of this with a house full of visitors asking the same questions. Groups of compassionate friends, family and church folk were reaching out during this terrible time when we just wanted to crawl into a hole somewhere. And when each new group arrived, there were the same questions, the retelling of what happened over and over again. Dark clouds began to gather around us as we attempted to handle our grief. How Satan loves to hit you when you are weak, defenseless and exhausted.

There are different ways of dealing with grief. Counselors write books about grief as if everyone were the same and dealt with the loss of a loved one the same way. During the time of crisis it is hard to listen to everyone's instruction and guidance. It is best to be forewarned and forearmed. This is why I am sharing my point of view to assist others in advance of their loss. From my perspective, there were 5 basic stages in the grief process:

- **Shock/denial**: These two are cousins and work closely together. Most have difficulty handling the pain that floods the soul when loss is experienced. Normally, the body acts as a buffer to deaden the pain and the coping system just shuts down. These responses are designed to help us recover and gain strength so that we might regain control. This too shall pass: a time will come when these two will relinquish their hold on the mind, the will, and the emotions; but without moral and spiritual support, shock and denial may return and once again overwhelm the raw emotions related to the loss of a loved one.

- **Anger**: Great personal loss can push anyone out of control and raw emotions become expressed in anger. We may be angry at God for permitting the loss to happen, or we may even feel anger toward the person who passed away for leaving us. We certainly can become angry at the people who may have caused the accident or medical workers who didn't do enough to save the loved one. We can also become angry at ourselves: perhaps we should have done more. If only we had been there... this would not have happened. Maybe we could have prayed more earnestly or had more faith. Anger is a natural emotion, but it must be controlled, especially in an emotional situation. Otherwise, anger can become a destructive force and a personal enemy of the soul. Anger stokes the fires of resentment and hardens our emotions and leads us away from healing so desperately needed in dealing with the loss of a loved one.

- **Longing**: This stage can be ruthless, especially when our days are filled with longing for the lost loved one. We forget that in only rare exceptions of Divine intervention death is not final. We remember the raising of Lazarus of Bethany (John 11:17) and want God to do the same in our situation. But situations are never the same because our thoughts are consumed by what will never be. We long to have our loved one back and no one or nothing else can fill that void. We long for life to be "normal" again, which means having the loved one back in our lives. Longing becomes the new "presence" in our life; it is always there and nothing deflects our focus away from what is missing in our life. At times this absence causes us to forget the bad and remember only the good in the life of our loved one: this is the good side of longing and can be part of the healing process that brings acceptance of God's will.

- **Acceptance**: the longing phase of grief can bring us to the difficult stage of acceptance. Some have estimated that accepting the loss of a child can take up to eight (8) years. Acceptance is not healing; it is the logical step that must be taken for the healing process to work. Acceptance of a loved one's death is necessary to move along the process of getting on with life. When this stage finally comes, we have most likely moved back and forth through the previous stages many times: longing and then back into denial. Perhaps angry and longing at the same time, but with patience, acceptance will finally come. For some, their minds and emotions have allowed a darkness to engulf their lives where the light of this stage will never shine. They have given into the darkness and do not intend to accept what they cannot change. Their lives shut down and revolve around their loss. They become isolated and withdrawn. Depression has bonded with the darkness to form a mighty millstone pulling them into the sea of despair.

- **Healing**: this final stage is one that is a long-term process. For most parents that lose a child, this process will be life-long. They will come to terms with their loss, and finally accept that they cannot bring their loved one back. This opens the door to reentering life. There may be times when the "longing stage" will resurface, but the cycle will become less often. For believers, this stage will lead their faith to embrace that God knows best. Provided the loved one was a believer, they will see them again. This hope tends to strengthen their resolve toward living their lives for Christ's honor.

With each of these stages comes a new set of issues to deal with. For instance, when the shock/denial stage begins to wear off, you then have to contend with a tidal wave of feelings. With the longing stage, by this time, the tears may be gone. When you were angry or even in shock, you could cry, but now the tears may just dry up. Bill went through that himself. At first, he cried often and deeply, but after a period of time, the tears just seemed to disappear. It wasn't that his emotions were hardened; it was as if he were so exhausted that he couldn't cry. Each stage will offer a different set of challenges. But these challenges must be faced and dealt with honestly and maturely. If not, healing is postponed.

Many believers go through the thought process that they are supposed to exhibit strength and not show weakness. Surely weakness would signal a lack of being spiritual, so they try to push aside their feelings and put on a mask. In doing so, they surrender their identity to just being religious. This falsehood does not give us opportunity to be human, to move through the different stages of grief because we appear to be in total control. The appearance of strength, of living our lives as if nothing affects our faith is also one that does not bring honor to our Savior. God's Word states that we comfort others whereby we have been comforted ourselves. How can we be used of God to comfort others when we have not allowed God to comfort us?

Sorry to say, but men are especially prone to this type of thought process. They want to be strong for their families, they do not want people feeling sorry for them and they want to be known for being a man of character. So they fall into the trap of shutting down their feelings and pushing forward as if nothing has happened. Yet inside, they cannot tame the emotions that they are privately struggling with. Their doubts, fears and anxieties are out of control and in turn create more pressure on them to gain control before others see through their mask. This terrible cycle leaves them empty, frustrated and feeling alone.

What is the best response to the loss of a loved one? First, we have to be honest with ourselves and others within our support network. Lying to yourself and to those around you only slows the process which leads to acceptance and healing. We must face the truth about our loss and what that loss means to us personally. We cannot just look at the loss from a perspective of "the family" or our mate or even our children. We have to face that loss personally, for how it impacts our life.

Second, we need people that we can be completely open with about our circumstance. Do not hold back those raw emotions but verbalize them, get them out in the open. By openly sharing your feelings with someone you trust, you create an outlet for those emotions and they do not explode. This gives us opportunity to put into words what we are thinking and feeling. When we hold thoughts and feelings inside, they lead to anger and depression. By voicing thoughts and emotions, we give the Holy Spirit opportunity to work within our hearts, and assist our understanding of the situation. By getting the hurt into the open, there is greater understanding of those hidden areas of pain that we are afraid to confront. The words of Rabbi Joshua Liebman are appropriate here:

> The melody that the loved one played upon the piano of your life will never be played quite that way again, but we must not close the keyboard and allow the instrument to gather dust. We must seek out other artists of the spirit, new friends who gradually will help us to find the road of life again, who will walk that road with us.

Third, don't put your focus totally on yourself or on your loved ones who are going through this loss. Focusing on yourself and your own pain only makes you more separated from others and alone with your pain. Focus must move away from your pain and must be applied to areas of acceptance and living, not just on death. Through each of the stages of grief, the focus has been on the death of the loved one. In order for there to be acceptance and healing, there must be a focus on life. Basically, we must take our eyes off the negative that has consumed us and place our sight back onto the positive aspects of life. What does this mean? We have to reaffirm God's purpose for our lives. We were created to glorify God and enjoy Him forever. We were created to fulfill His purpose. Our lives were not meant to become a monument to the past or to a loved one that has passed.

Fourth, as we take our sight off of the pain and grief, we begin rebuilding a relationship with our Heavenly Father. For many believers, this relationship will take a backseat to the pain and loss. During times of terrible grief, we lose proper contact with the Savior through the Holy Spirit. For me, it was more about listening to God than it was about talking to God. There were many times I just did not know what to say. When I did raise my voice to God, it was more about arguing with God or blaming God for allowing my loved one to be taken from me. After all, God certainly had the power to save her and give her back to us, but He chose otherwise. Our spiritual life demanded that we accept God's wisdom and will for our lives and reopen our spiritual lives to positive contact with Him.

Early into the grief process you must learn to be quiet and just sit before the Lord with an open heart. The Word states: "Be still and know that I am God." Being still is a great opportunity to let the Holy Spirit comfort you, to permit your mind and emotions to sort through all the confusion and pain. Too many times we enter into prayer with the only objective being to share with God what we need and what we want. This should not be the believer's sole purpose in prayer and it should never be our purpose when we are grieving. We need time to engage in the silent side of prayer and listen to God and understand what He has to say to our hearts.

Several months ago, my grandson, Dylan, spoke to me about the nature of a hurricane. Normally in the center of the storm (the eye), it is calm, clear and cloud free. The storm is raging all around the eye of the storm, but those in the eye of the storm are safe, at least for a while. Jesus is in the eye of the storm for believers. We go through many storms in life so there is a great need to learn to permit Christ to speak in a "still small voice" in the center of each storm, so we can find peace and safety in His presence.

We must be still and know that God loves us and He is the God we have known in our past experiences and He is the same God of this present circumstance. I have learned that being still and calm is a process enabled by the Holy Spirit. In the midst of the storm, we must put our "hand in the hand of the Man that can say "Peace be still!" We must hang on to His hand for security. I have found that Jesus is my greatest security; it is He alone who cannot be moved by the greatest storms. Personal and spiritual strength does not depend on what we can do, but what Christ can do in us and through us when we yield our will to Him.   It is during these times when we will realize with C. S. Lewis *I need Christ, not something that resembles Him.*

Fifth, with the loss of a loved one, we tend to focus our thoughts and emotions only on the past. Taking our eyes off the past is one of the most difficult areas that we must deal with in grief. We long for the time when the loved one was so much a part of our life. If we are to begin living again, we must focus on Jesus – He is able to strengthen our spiritual life for the journey. He is the beginning and the end...He knows the end from the beginning. We must permit Him to guide each forward step toward eternity. The end is worth the journey regardless of human difficulties and hardships we face along the way. There we will "know as we were known" meaning we will both see and be with loved ones who have gone before. That "glad reunion day" is just ahead....we can almost see the lights of the City!

Oh, I can almost see the lights of that city;
I see them gathering all around the great white throne.
Through faith in my Savior and His wonderful love.
Oh, I can almost see the lights of home.
—Belinda Johnson

Yes, the future is bright, but God did not design His grace for the future, but for the present. Focusing on the past or focusing solely on the future keeps us from living the "now" and fulfilling the present duties to which God called and anointed us. God does not want us to focus entirely on either the past or the future. God's grace can help us to heal in the present and be ready to support others because of our experience. To live or dwell in the past is to live where we have already walked. God's purpose for our life is one of progress, not retreat. Retreating into the past or by passing the present so that we might live out our life in depression by focusing only on the future will never bring glory to our Lord's name. Hebrews 12:2 tells us to look unto Jesus, the Author and Finisher of our faith. We began this walk of faith in Christ and it is Christ that will guide us to the finish line!

Sixth, once we have settled quietly before our Lord, we must move toward His Word. The Word of God is the greatest tool we have in gaining understanding and knowledge needed to live our lives and fulfill God's purpose. Death has taken us completely off course and God's Word must be utilized to regain direction on that course. There is no substitute for God's Word in any circumstance of life. During a period of mourning the loss of a loved one, your mind and emotions may be so overwhelmed that you may seem disconnected from God's Word. Always remember when you were first saved and how you struggled to understand what the Word was saying. During great loss, you may enter a period where it may seem the same way again. Keep taking in and digesting His Word and keep praying for the Holy Spirit to grant you wisdom and understanding. It is not about how much you read; it is about hearing what God is saying to you each day. That is why times of silence before God when you read His Word is vital to recover from grief. Learn afresh the lessons of grace in the Word. Learn to treasure the Word and the Holy Spirit will complete His work within you.

If you have experienced the death of a child as I did, please know that since you are God's child, He is there for you and stands with you. He will never abandon you, never leave you without help and He will never give up on you! I have learned in my own life that He can be trusted even with the most precious area of my life: the death of a child.

EPILOGUE

Looking Down the Path

May my life touch a dozen lives.
Before this day is done.
Leave countless marks for good, not ill,
Before sets the evening sun.
So this is the wish I always desire,
The prayer I continually pray:
"Lord may my life help others,
It touches by the way."

—Marie Green Pogue
(1972)

When I consider the guiding light of the Word, it encourages me to remember the God I serve is with me presently and is guiding me each step of the way. As I move closer to the final chapter of my life's story, I am compelled to look down the path to the next steps and know the light of the Word will show me the way forward. My present steps as well as the next phase of my life, are directed by this verse, *Thy word is a lamp unto my feet, and a light unto my path.* (Psalms 19: 105). The first part, ***Thy word is a lamp unto my feet***, speaks of God giving me light for my current walk. This means the Word of God is lighting the steps of my daily walk on life's journey.

Think about this marvelous moment: God is showing me where I am right now and shinning His light on my pathway so I will see clearly the next steps of my journey! The last part of the verse, *a light unto my path*, means God will guide me continually each step of my journey. When I meditate on this reality, it encourages me to remember the God I serve is with me presently and is guiding each step forward. What does this show me about the latest phase of my life? It means God is in control of my life that is being written daily. He is the Lord of my life, not only of the past, but the present and my future area of ministry to others. God is giving me light and I am seeing a little distance down the road. What is that light showing me? That God has a plan and purpose for my life, not just for today, but for the rest of my life! And He also has a purpose for you now and for the rest of your life, too!

God has been leading me step by step into a compassionate ministry to women; to help others, just like myself, that have daily problems and everyday roadblocks to what God wants their lives to be. I have felt this sense of calling in my life and God has consistently opened doors for me to speak to women in groups and to assist others one-on-one. I certainly believe this ministry is an enormous part of what God has in store for this phase in my life. **And a light unto my path**, speaks clearly of what is coming down the road. If I were to take a lamp out on a dark night and walk down a path, that light would allow me to see right around me but it would also give me enough light to see a short distance on down the path. That is what God is saying to me in this part of the verse. He is giving me light for the now, but He is also giving each of us light for our tomorrows and even further on down the road.

God does not want any of us wandering through life without a sense of direction. He wants us traveling a purposeful journey, headed in the right direction and walking always in accordance with His will. Throughout my journey thus far, I have learned that my emergency is God's priority.

Recently, I have embraced an additional goal……. creating my own bucket list; that is, list all the things I want to do before I kick the bucket! As I grow older and witness more of God's grace, I have decided to survey my life and list all the things I wanted to do, but either did not have the time, money or health to do. Now, I'm going to open up my life, try some new things and allow God to show me mighty and marvelous things! Have you ever wanted to reach outside your comfort zone and let go and let God? To just let God have control of your life and allow Him to take you to spiritual places that you have never experienced before? That is what I want to do in this "second half" of my life!

When you have health problems hanging over your head, you feel limited and restrained, and realize you are missing so much. Not sinful things, but the good things in life. I believe God's grace can take me to places that are presently unknown. I want to experience God with family and friends where the Word of God states that *God has made us to sit together in heavenly places*. I want to go there, to those heavenly places and experience everything humanly possible that God has promised believers. I want a fresh relationship with God, an experience that takes me where I have never been before. I want a connection with God similar to Moses on the mountain when his image glowed with heavenly glory! Think about sitting where God sits and walking where God walks, I want to go beyond the restraints of normality and live where God lives! Think of the possibilities in such a place. To see women truly overcome their fears, their doubts, their insecurities and their loss of self-esteem. That is where I want to go, and by God's grace, I'll get there!

My husband taught the church, *Where no counsel is, the people fall: but in the multitude of counselors there is safety* (Proverbs 11:14). In interpreting this verse, it fits well with what I have in mind concerning where God has called me. It states, *Where no guidance or steering is, the people fall: but in the multitude of those that give guidance, there is deliverance.* What the Word teaches here is that God wants us to have guidance and be steered in the right direction. He accomplishes this through three primary means:

The work of the Holy Spirit,

The Word of God, and

Counselors and teachers of His Word.

Are you making use of all these instruments in your life? The Holy Spirit, God's Word and counselors/Bible teachers are all used by God to keep us from stumbling spiritually. God does not want us to stagger at His promises and not follow His guidance, but desires that we live victoriously and walk in the power of the Holy Spirit!

My present desire for this phase of life is to be used by God as a human instrument of grace to reach other women in need of guidance. My desire is to lead them to a safe place of deliverance from the issues that bog down their lives! To be free of those things that limit them and that have been obstacles of spiritual and physical defeat in their lives.

It has been such a joy to share a little about my life with you through the pages of this book. My prayer for each one who reads my story is that they know the incredible God I serve. Again I join Saint Paul and say that the adversities of this life are not worthy to be compared to the joy God has in store for the overcomer. His marvelous grace is sufficient for you! May I remind each of you that He is above all and is Lord of all. My deepest wish is that His Name be glorified through all the days of my life and yours as well. That is my heart's desire! — *Miss Kay*

WALKING WITH MISS KAY

AFTERWORD

There are no crown-wearers in heaven who were not cross-bearers here below.

—Charles Haddon Spurgeon

Several years ago, our Sunday school class went to a local retreat. Three or four of us were responsible for the lesson and devotion. At that time, I did not know Kay as I know her now. We had only been together a couple of years. When she spoke to us, God touched my heart. I heard a shy, withdrawn person come forward with strength and confidence. She spoke with knowledge and surety, confident and full of love for her Heavenly Father. I knew then that God had a special place for her and could use her greatly.

Shortly after the retreat, I mentioned to her about teaching a ladies class. I told her I felt God's hand on this work. At first she smiled and said she would pray about it. Several months went by. I could not forget her confidence, her authority in the Word of God. A lot of prayer and several months later, she accepted the call to teach the ladies class at New Life Baptist Church.

Many years and three transplants later, she is still with us. God's anointing on her has spilled over to our class numerous times. His touch on our class, His anointing is something to experience. She is a willing vessel and that is all that He asks from any of us. Thank you, God, for the revelation of your grace and the answer to our prayers.

—Xavia Depew, Choir Director,
New Life Baptist Church

ABOUT THE AUTHORS

Bill and Kay Christian were high school sweethearts and will celebrate 40 years of marriage this year. They have three children: Amber, Adena "Dee", and Dylan, as well as several grandchildren.

Bill and Kay were the founders of Hope Bible Camp, a ministry to handicapped children in East Tennessee and Southwest Virginia.

Kay is a former deaf education interpreter working in all levels of education. She started her career in middle school, then moved to elementary and finished up her career interpreting at East Tennessee State University and Northeast State University. Kay's primary ministry focus is speaking to women's groups and churches throughout the region conveying the lessons of hope and perseverance that she learned while walking with Jesus.

Bill, a former evangelist, has been the Sr. Pastor of New Life Baptist Church in Bluff City, Tennessee for the past 21 years. The mission statement of the church Bill and Kay serve sums up the focus of their ministry:

Love God, love others, and live to serve.

WALKING WITH MISS KAY

ISBN 978-1-935434-68-9

Order through

www.gea-books.com

or

Amazon.com, BarnesAndNoble.com

Email: GlobalEdAdvance@aol.com

or any bookstore may order books through Ingram.

GREEN WINE FAMILY BOOKS

a division of
GlobalEdAdvance Press